Fruitful

'But the fruit of the Spirit is love, joy, peace, patience, kindness, goodness, faithfulness, gentleness and self-control.' Gal. 5:22-23

Selwyn Hughes
Revised and updated by Mick Brooks
FURTHER STUDY: IAN SEWTER

© CWR 2016. Dated text previously published as *Every Day with Jesus: The Harvest of the Spirit* (September/October 2004) by CWR. This edition revised and updated for 2016 by Mick Brooks. Pages on prayer (21–25 September 2016) written by Mick Brooks, in support of the National Prayer Weekend 2016.

CWR, Waverley Abbey House, Waverley Lane, Farnham, Surrey GU9 8EP, UK **Tel: 01252 784700**
Email: mail@cwr.org.uk Registered Charity No. 294387. Registered Limited Company No. 1990308.

Cover image: stocksy.com/zocky
Quiet Time image: Fotosearch
Printed in England by Linney Print

MIX
Paper from responsible sources
FSC® C015900

A word of introduction ...

As children of the living God, prayer is one of our key roles. Another is being His ambassadors. In all this He does not leave us floundering. He graciously sent His Holy Spirit to help us grow, live peaceably and be fruitful in our relationships with one another and the world. Imagine the impact if we displayed the nine qualities of the fruit of the Spirit in our lives fully. It could turn the world upside down, painting a clear picture of what it means to be a Christian and live the Christian life. In the weeks ahead, it's my prayer that, as you allow the Holy Spirit to work in your life, you will become ever more fruitful.

CWR was founded by Selwyn Hughes with the vision to encourage people to pray for both personal and national revival, and deepen their understanding of the Word of God. Selwyn always believed that one of the calls on his life was to help the Church to focus on revival. Our task, he used to say, is to provide the 'prayer-ramp' over which God's purposes can pass.

This September we are once again encouraging as many as churches and people as possible, not just in the UK but all around the world, to participate in the National Prayer Weekend 2016. It's not too late to join in and gather requests from family, friends, neighbours, local businesses, schools – anyone in your local community – and bring their requests before our loving heavenly Father on their behalf.

Mick Brooks, Consulting Editor

Mick

Please join us on the **23–25 September** and take part in the National Prayer Weekend 2016. For more information, visit **www.national-prayer-weekend.com**

As fruit in an orchard

FOR READING & MEDITATION - GALATIANS 5:13-26

'The fruit of the Spirit is love, joy, peace, patience, kindness, goodness, faithfulness, gentleness and self-control.' (vv22-23)

Today we begin a devotional exploration of the fruit of the Spirit – the nine qualities that go to make up Christian character. Eugene Peterson, in *The Message*, paraphrases this passage beautifully: 'God … brings gifts into our lives, much the same way that fruit appears in an orchard – things like affection for others, exuberance about life, serenity. We develop a willingness to stick with things, a sense of compassion in the heart, and a conviction that a basic holiness permeates things and people. We find ourselves involved in loyal commitments, not needing to force our way in life, able to marshal and direct our energies wisely.'

John Stott once said that Galatians 5:22–23 were his favourite verses in the Bible, and that he meditated on these verses more than any others. May I suggest as a helpful spiritual exercise over the next two months that you repeat these verses to yourself every day. You may be surprised at what happens.

Before going any further it is important to notice that when Paul speaks about the things that originate from our sinful nature in Galatians 5:19–21 he calls them 'acts', but when talking about the qualities that develop from the Spirit he calls them 'fruit'. 'Acts' points to something manufactured whereas 'fruit' suggests something that grows without effort – an outcome of the Spirit abiding within. The Church would be transformed if every Christian developed the nine qualities listed in this passage. We would not need to pray for revival because the wonderful signs of revival would already be apparent. People of the world would come knocking at our door wanting to learn how to live.

FURTHER STUDY

Gen. 1:26-29; 2:8-17

1. What is the purpose of natural fruit (relate your answer to spiritual fruit)?

2. What was Adam's responsibility?

My Father and my God, give me a fresh vision and desire to grow in my life every characteristic of the fruit of the Spirit so that more of Jesus may be seen in me. In His name I pray. Amen.

Becoming a better person

FOR READING & MEDITATION - JOHN 15:12-17

'I chose you and appointed you to go and bear fruit –
fruit that will last' (v16)

Imparting the qualities listed in Galatians 5:22–23 is just one aspect of the Spirit's work in the life of a Christian. Though this may be regarded by some as an oversimplification, it may be said that the Holy Spirit seeks to minister to us in two particular ways: to make us more pure and to develop in us spiritual maturity. That maturity is conferred through the gifts of the Spirit and purity through the fruit that we are exploring in this issue. The two, I would say, are of equal importance.

Many Christians claim that they are far more interested in the fruit of the Spirit than the gifts, but that is not what God desires. He longs for us to be a people who demonstrate both maturity and purity. So please be assured that in emphasising the fruit of the Spirit I have not intended to divert attention from the gifts of the Spirit and their miraculous nature or to put one before the other.

FURTHER STUDY

2 Cor. 3:13-18;
Gal. 1:13-24

1. What is the outcome of our transformation?

2. What was the result of Paul's transformation?

The indwelling of the Holy Spirit results in many things, and one of the most important is a quality of being – a quality of being that has nine characteristics. A number of biblical translations use the term 'harvest of the Spirit' rather than 'fruit of the Spirit', pointing to the finished product, the outcome. When we allow the Holy Spirit to take root in our hearts then the fruit produced is the nine qualities listed in Galatians 5:22–23. As the Holy Spirit resides within us we do not just become the recipients of pleasurable emotions, though of course that does happen. The divine indwelling makes us better people. We must never forget that God's primary concern is that we might become holy – but remember the holier we are the happier we will be.

God my Father, help me right here at the beginning to get my focus right and live, not simply for better feelings, but to be a better person. In Jesus' name I ask it. Amen.

The primacy of love

FOR READING & MEDITATION - 1 CORINTHIANS 13:1-13

'And now these three remain: faith, hope and love.
But the greatest of these is love.' (v13)

The first fruit of the Spirit is 'love'. Love is the chief distinguishing mark of God's children. Some regard the chief mark of a Christian as faith. But today's reading says that even if we have faith that can move mountains but do not have love then we are nothing. Others say that truth is the greatest distinguishing mark of a Christian, but Paul tells us here that even if we can fathom all mysteries and understand the truth about everything yet do not have love then again we are nothing.

Paul's mention in Galatians 5:22 of love as the first fruit of the Spirit fits in with his teaching here in I Corinthians 13. Love, he claims, is greater than everything else – miracles, faith, service and so on. Examining I Corinthians 13 carefully we see that every fruit of the Spirit mentioned in Galatians 5 is linked somewhere with this quality of supernatural love; either directly or by the use of synonyms each of them is mentioned. Every other fruit proceeds from this first fruit of love. Notice the connection: love is patient – patience; love is kind – kindness; love does not envy – goodness; love does not boast and is not proud – gentleness; love is not self-seeking and is not easily angered – self-control and peace; love rejoices with the truth – joy; love always protects, always hopes, always perseveres – faithfulness.

FURTHER STUDY

Matt. 22:34-40;
Luke 10:29-37

1. What did Jesus prioritise?

2. How may this become a reality?

Once we have love, we have all the fruit of the Spirit. Without it we are nothing. Indeed, I would go further and say that not only is love the first outcome of the Spirit within but that if love is lacking then everything is lacking. If you have the Spirit you will have love; if you do not have love you do not have the Spirit.

Gracious Father, I see that whatever else I possess, if I do not possess love then I am nothing. Help me always be open to You so that love - Your love - may grow and be seen in me. Amen.

Mature – only in love

FOR READING & MEDITATION - EPHESIANS 4:7-16

'Instead, speaking the truth in love, we will in all things grow up into him who is the Head, that is, Christ.' (v15)

As we are seeing, love is the ultimate gift of God and is the very first evidence of the work of the Spirit within. If love is lacking then everything is lacking. I would say that the very first indication that we are growing spiritually is that we are growing in love. God's essential nature is love and, as we receive and rest in that love, changes occur and the other qualities begin to grow.

Our text today, in the Moffatt translation, tells us that we are to 'hold by the truth, and by our love to grow up wholly into Him'. There is only one way to grow up 'wholly into Him'

FURTHER STUDY

Eph. 3:14-21;
2 Thess. 1:1-3

1. Where should we be rooted?

2. What was Paul's commendation?

and that is 'by our love'. No matter how many good works we do, or how much of the Bible we know, we will remain spiritually immature if we are not developing in love. Some think that if they start to love themselves more then they are fulfilling the scriptural commands to love, but if the love is ingrown and focused on the self then God's design for the personality is being circumvented. We are to love as we are loved. Or if the love is selectively applied to certain groups then again we are misunderstanding Jesus' command to love (John 13:34–35). We are only mature to the extent that we can love and give out love to everybody. Indeed, any growth without growth in love is what has been described as 'sucker love' – growth that bears no fruit.

J.B. Phillips' translation of 1 Corinthians 8:1 describes the matter in this way: 'While knowledge may make a man look big, it is only love that can make him grow to his full stature.' Today – and rightly so – there is a growing emphasis on knowing more of the Bible. But knowledge of the Bible is not enough. It must be accompanied by love.

Father, I sense that You are bringing me to the very crux of things. May I see that if I am not growing in love then I am not growing in You. Help me to receive and rest in Your love. In Jesus' name I ask this. Amen.

Unconditional love

FOR READING & MEDITATION - 2 CORINTHIANS 5:11-21

'For Christ's love compels us, because we are convinced that one
died for all, and therefore all died.' (v14)

What exactly does Scripture mean when it uses the word
'love'? In English the word 'love' has such a variety of
meanings. It is used for the mighty passion that moves in
the heart of God but it is used also in connection with such
things as the flutterings of the heart, an extramarital affair,
even chocolate or sport. The one word 'love' has to cover a
multiplicity of diverse meanings.

The Greek language is much richer in this respect. It has
four words for love. One is *eros*, meaning love between the
sexes. Another is *philia*, meaning affectionate human love.
Then there is the word *storge*, meaning family love.
The most powerful word for love, however, is *agape*,
which means unconditional love – the love that
resides in the heart of God. Everything God does
is motivated by love. He can do nothing without
love being the controlling factor. When Paul says
in Galatians 5:22 that 'the fruit of the Spirit is love',
the word he uses for 'love' is *agape*. The love we are
invited to experience and demonstrate when we are
indwelt by the Spirit is not a general kind of love
but love of a specific kind – the love that swells in
the heart of God and is seen exemplified in Jesus.

**FURTHER
STUDY**

Hosea 6:4;
John 15:9-17

1. What was
God's criticism
of Israel's love
for Him?

2. What is
the ultimate
expression
of love?

In today's text Paul says, 'For Christ's love
compels us.' This cuts deep. It is possible to be
compelled by the love of achievement, of success, of a cause,
of a fight. Respectfully I ask: What compels you – the love
of a cause or the love of Christ? The enemies of the early
Christians complained that these followers of Jesus love
each other even before they are acquainted. They did. They
couldn't help it, for the very nature of the faith they had
embraced was love.

**Father God, as I examine my motives, may I see that I, like the
apostle Paul, can be compelled by the love of Christ. Please pour
Your love in so that I may pour it out to others. In Jesus' name.
Amen.**

Love cannot fail

FOR READING & MEDITATION - JOHN 13:18-38

'A new command I give you: Love one another. As I have loved you, so you must love one another.' (v34)

The love that flows in our hearts when we are indwelt by the Holy Spirit is not general but specific – the *agape* love of God. This love dulls the edge of disappointment and enables us to more maturely deal with many things, not least a lack of appreciation. Shakespeare was no doubt thinking of this high degree of love when he wrote Sonnet 116:

Love is not love,
Which alters when it alteration finds,
Or bends with the remover to remove.
Oh no! It is an ever fixed mark,
That looks on tempests and is never shaken.

FURTHER STUDY

Jer. 31:3-14;
Eph. 4:32-5:1

1. What is the chief characteristic of God's love?

2. How can we imitate God?

Let's follow this thought through a little more deeply. The nine qualities that are the fruit of the Spirit were all exemplified in Jesus' life on earth. It is the purpose of the Holy Spirit to nurture these qualities in us as we abide in Jesus and maintain a close, day-by-day relationship with Him. If we allow God to do this, what a tremendous difference it will make to our lives and communities. This is what God wants for us. To emphasise again, when we allow the Spirit to work in our lives the very first evidence of His presence is *agape* love. This is not a give-and-take kind of love, a love that is reciprocal; it is a love that descends from above and is showered on the deserving and the undeserving. Christians who dwell deeply in God find that they are changed from people who just love occasionally, when it is convenient, to people whose controlling purpose is love. Love becomes the compelling motive and passion in their lives.

Agape love never fails for, even though it may not always have an effect on others and change them, it most definitely affects us. We are the better for loving.

Father, I see that by expressing love I become more loving even when the other person doesn't accept my love. I cannot fail in love even if love seems to fail in accomplishing the desired end. I am so thankful. Amen.

CWR Ministry Events

PLEASE PRAY FOR THE TEAM

DATE	EVENT	PLACE	PRESENTER(S)
Sep	Mentoring Others	Waverley Abbey House	Andy Peck
Sep	Understanding Yourself, Understanding Others	WAH	Jeanette Barwick
Sep	Prayer Breakfast	Pilgrim Hall	Pilgrim Hall team
Sep	Church Leaders Forum	WAH	Andy Peck
–25 Sep	Inspiring Women Autumn Weekend: In His Strength	WAH	Lynn Penson and Lynette Brooks
Sep	Hearing God's Voice	WAH	Andy Peck
Oct	Inspiring Women Autumn Day: Digging for Diamonds	WAH	Cathy Madavan and the Inspiring Women team
Oct	What Jesus Says about Leading	WAH	Andy Peck
Oct	Closing the Back Door: Revisited	WAH	Andy Peck
14 Oct	Woman to Woman Training Course	WAH	Inspiring Women team
Oct	Insight into Assertiveness	WAH	Chris Ledger
Oct	Ready Answers	WAH	Andy Peck
23 Oct	Bible Discovery Weekend: The Prophet Ezekiel	WAH	Philip Greenslade
Oct	Boundaries	WAH	Kara Lawman and team
–28 Oct	Autumn Retreat	PH	Pilgrim Hall team
Oct	Pastoral Care Today	WAH	Andy Peck
–29 Oct	Transforming Love	WAH	Liz Babbs

Please pray for our ongoing ministry in Singapore and Cambodia. In particular, for our tutors Ron Kallmier and Lizzy Jakeman as they present part three of our counselling course in Singapore on the 1–3 and 8–10 September, and in Cambodia on the 5–8 September. They will then be teaching part four of the course on the 27–29 October and 3–4 November in Singapore, and 31 October – 3 November in Cambodia.

For further information and a full list of CWR's courses, phone **+44 (0)1252 784719** or visit the CWR website **www.cwr.org.uk**

You can also download our free daily Prayer Track from **www.cwr.org.uk/free-resources**

The blinding revelation

FOR READING & MEDITATION - LUKE 23:32-46

'When they came to the place called the Skull, they crucified him
there, along with the criminals' (v33)

How can we ensure that the love that resides in the heart of God resides in our hearts also? Well, we cannot force ourselves to love or attempt to manufacture it in our hearts. We simply allow God to love within us. In my experience those who best manifest God's love are those who have had a blinding realisation of the love of God and their own love flames in response. But how do we come to have such a realisation? There is only one way this can happen. It is to go to the foot of the cross. Here, and only here, is the heart of God fully unveiled.

FURTHER STUDY

Phil. 2:1-8;
Rom. 5:1-8

1. What indignities did Jesus suffer for love?

2. How has God clearly proved and demonstrated His love?

From childhood we may have been familiar with the text 'God is love' (1 John 4:8), and after a while it has no more effect on us than the knowledge that the sun rises every morning in the East and sets in the West – it is simply part of the order of things. There is no wonder in it, and no realisation either. Then one day we stand at the foot of the cross, look up into the face of Jesus, and the Spirit reveals the love of God to our hearts in such a way that the scales fall from our eyes and we are transformed. This is not a natural occurrence; it is supernatural. It happens in direct proportion to our desire to know more of God and His love. When that transformation takes place, the truth we have known all our lives from an intellectual point of view – that God is love – takes hold of us and for the first time ever we come to a full realisation of it.

Permit once again a personal question: Has there been a moment in your life when you have been 'blinded' by the love of God? Ask God today to give you a fresh revelation and experience of His *agape* love.

Father, how can I become fully aware of Your love unless You reveal it to me? As I sit in contemplation before Calvary, let Your love take hold of me afresh. In Jesus' name I pray. Amen.

FOR READING & MEDITATION - 1 JOHN 4:7-21

'This is love: not that we loved God, but that he loved us and sent his Son as an atoning sacrifice for our sins.' (v10)

When we begin to live in the good of how much God loves us, an amazing change is brought about in our personalities and we start to love like Him. We cannot help it. Love – *agape* love – is not the fruit of labour – it is a response. When we stand at the foot of the cross, the place where the love of God was expressed most fully, the scales fall from our eyes and, as I said earlier, our own love flames in response. We love because we are loved, says the apostle John. Love originates not with us but with God.

Teresa of Avila once described how one day, going into her room, she noticed a picture of Jesus being scourged before His crucifixion. She must have seen the picture hundreds of times before, but in that moment of revelation she saw it as she had never seen it before. She saw God suffering – suffering out of love and suffering for her. The revelation sent her to her knees, sobbing in wonder, and when she arose she was a changed woman. The revelation of Calvary's love was the great divide in her life. She said that she arose with a sense of 'unpayable debt' and went out to share what she now realised about God's love with others.

Never try to manufacture love. Linger in the shadow of the cross. Spend time focusing on Calvary and what happened there. The love of God finds its most burning expression at the cross. Meditate on it. Contemplate it. Remember that heaven knows no higher strategy for pouring love into human hearts than by granting us a vision of how much we are loved – a vision strong enough to evoke a response in our hearts. And when we respond to that love, it begins to grow in us and through us.

FURTHER STUDY

John 3:16;
Rom. 8:31-39;
Gal. 2:20;
Eph. 2:1-9

1. What was Paul's revelation of God's love?

2. How does his use of personal pronouns show his personal revelation?

Gracious Father, slowly the truth is sinking in - before I can love, I must understand how much I am loved. Increase my understanding still further, dear Lord. In Jesus' name I ask it. Amen.

Always a reason to rejoice

FOR READING & MEDITATION – PSALM 105:1-15

'Let the hearts of those who seek the LORD rejoice.' (v3)

Now we move on to consider the second fruit of the Spirit – joy or, as *The Message* version expresses it, 'an exuberance about life'. It is not by accident that joy follows love because joy is a by-product of love. If you focus on finding joy it will elude you. But if you concentrate on finding love then joy will seek you out, as the natural outcome of love is an exuberance about life. Again let's remember that the nine qualities that are the fruit of the Spirit are not natural attributes but supernatural ones. We cannot manufacture them; they grow and develop in our lives as we allow the Holy Spirit to work within us.

FURTHER STUDY

Isa. 35:1-10;
Heb. 12:1-2

1. What happens when God comes to save?

2. Why did Jesus endure the cross?

Sadly many Christians find it difficult to accept that joy is a fruit of the Spirit. And not only do they not expect joy – they believe we shouldn't want it. A grim Christian once told me, 'At the heart of our faith is a cross. This means we ought to be spending our time weeping, not laughing.' Well, it is true that the cross is at the heart of the Christian faith and that following Jesus is at times difficult, but this is set against the fact that the second fruit of the Spirit is joy. No one can deny that from time to time each of us has to face suffering. However, a Christian possesses a subterranean spring of joy that will, if we allow it, burst upwards even in times of struggle and difficulties. Joy, like love, is the essence of our faith. The empty tomb takes away our empty gloom. We have an Easter morning to celebrate in our faith, and that means there is always a reason to rejoice.

Friends, as we are open to God's love, the other fruits of the Spirit, including joy, will grow in the soil of our hearts naturally.

Father, I am so grateful that Your Holy Spirit touches my life at the deepest level, which means I can experience joy even in the midst of struggles. Thank You, dear Father. Amen.

Walking the glory road

FOR READING & MEDITATION - PSALM 30:1-12

'Weeping may remain for a night, but rejoicing comes in the morning.'
(v5)

Joy, we are saying, is one of the chief outcomes of the Christian life, and yet sadly many believers seem to know nothing of it. This is a great hindrance to our witness. One woman used to give out gospel literature at a railway station, but her face did not express the joy the literature talked about. Seeing this, one person handed back the literature saying, 'No thank you. I've enough troubles of my own.' One Christian once described a fellow believer who was failing to experience joy as 'creaking in body and soul as he limps along the highway towards glory'. This joyless soul was walking the road to glory but did not appear to be walking the glory road.

The Greek word *chara*, translated 'joy', is a robust word. It is exuberant and overflowing. The summons to rejoice is sounded no less than seventy times in the New Testament, and the word *chara* occurs close on sixty times. The New Testament really is a book of joy.

I recall reading once that joy is the distinctive atmosphere of the Christian life; that whatever the ingredients (and their proportions) of the Christian experience, joy is certainly mixed in. Even in the days after the death of my wife, I was wonderfully conscious of joy quietly percolating through the layers of my sadness and grief. Joy is always present in the hearts of those who know God. It may not always be felt or recognised, but it is always there. And eventually it will break through to the surface, no matter what our situation or our circumstances. As a young preacher I always maintained that joy is inevitably part of the Christian life. Now experience proves it.

FURTHER STUDY

Psa. 16:1-11; 30:10-12; 126:1-6

1. Contrast those who seek the Lord with those who run after other gods.

2. How does God restore our fortunes?

Father, thank You for reminding me that when joy has its roots in You then its fruits will eventually appear - no matter what happens. All glory and honour be to Your name. Amen.

Joy - more than pleasure

FOR READING & MEDITATION - JOHN 16:17-33

'Now is your time of grief, but I will see you again and you will rejoice, and no-one will take away your joy.' (v22)

One reason why large numbers of Christians do not experience the benefits of spiritual joy, we suggested the other day, is because they do not expect to. When one woman experienced Christian conversion she commented, 'It's strange, but I never associated joy with God before.' How sad that so many think joy is something reserved for the hereafter and do not expect their faith to make them joyful now. Yet, as we see from today's text, Jesus explained to the disciples that joy is part of our present experience here in this environment spoiled by sin.

FURTHER STUDY

Acts 5:40-42;
16:22-25;
2 Cor. 6:3-10

1. How did the apostles respond to persecution?

2. What was Paul's experience?

We can better understand this God-given joy if we distinguish it from the pleasures of life with which it is sometimes confused. God-given joy is quite different from pleasure or happiness. Anyone can experience pleasure and happiness but the rich and deep exuberance about life received from God is another matter. Indeed, people in this world often pride themselves on knowing how to experience pleasure. Yet pleasure and Christian joy are definitely different. Let's look together at one of the main differences, which we first explored in the March/April issue.

Pleasure depends on circumstances. It requires conditions to be favourable and thus it can be stolen from us by things like lack of money – or even such a minor matter as a toothache. Christian joy, however, is completely independent of circumstances. It is there in the believer even when strength and health and friends are gone – when circumstances are not only unkind but savage. It is wonderful to see Jesus' exuberant joy burst forth even in those who are caught up in pain or persecution. That joy can prove triumphant is not just a theory but a glorious fact.

Father, how can I thank You enough for imparting into my sadness Your unconquerable gladness? No matter what happens, all is well with my soul. I am so grateful. Amen.

Changing pleasures

FOR READING & MEDITATION - HEBREWS 13:1-16

'Jesus Christ is the same yesterday and today and for ever.' (v8)

Yesterday we said that pleasure depends on circumstances and Christian joy does not. Another difference is this: pleasures come and go. Look back over your life for a moment and think of the different things that have given you pleasure over the years. Perhaps, when you were a child, it was a bicycle that brought you pleasure. Or a football. Or a doll. Then, when you entered your teens, it was something else. A relationship, perhaps, or a sport. In later years the things that gave you pleasure changed again. The theatre, books, an armchair … the things that give us pleasure change over the years. But the joy of God is constant. Speaking of joy, I once heard someone say, 'Children may know it, it can be the strong stay of youth, the means by which the middle aged may bear the heat and burden of the day and the secret exultation of those who grow old.'

FURTHER STUDY

Neh. 8:9-10;
Hab. 3:17-19

1. What are the characteristics of a sacred day?

2. Why was Habakkuk's joy independent of circumstances?

Yet another difference between pleasure and joy is this: pleasure satiates. It is easy to have too much. And when the point of satiety is passed a sense of complacency can set in. The things for which we once craved become mundane to us and we look for something different to bring us pleasure. Joy, however, never satiates. A Christian may say, 'We have enough, yet not too much to long for more.'

One more difference between pleasure and joy is that pleasure is often superficial and, as we have said, depends on circumstances. The joy that is the fruit of the Spirit, however, remains with us constantly – even in times of sorrow, as Paul could testify (2 Cor. 6:10). We may not immediately sense it or feel it but it is there supporting and holding us and will eventually break through.

Gracious Father, fill me afresh with Your joy, as I know that it goes so much deeper than physical circumstances. And help me to radiate Your joy wherever I go. In Jesus' name I ask it. Amen.

Help prisoners know God's Word

Each year CWR provides over 60,000 free Bible reading notes to prisoners. Daily engagement with the Bible changes lives. We need your help to answer the many requests for these notes from prisoners eager to know more of God ...

'Daily readings are an important part of my faith. I only wish I had read more in the past. God is truly blessing me with freedom, despite being behind bars.'

'One of the criminals who hung there hurled insults at him: "Aren't you the Messiah? Save yourself and us!"
But the other criminal rebuked him. "Don't you fear God," he said, "since you are under the same sentence? We are punished justly, for we are getting what our deeds deserve. But this man has done nothing wrong."
Then he said, "Jesus, remember me when you come into your kingdom."
Jesus answered him, "Truly I tell you, today you will be with me in paradise."'

(Luke 23:39-43)

The criminal on the cross is an incredible example of forgiveness in the face of suffering, demonstrating how God has the power to completely change someone's life.

Today, this same truth is experienced in hundreds of prisons worldwide. Prisoners are faced with reflecting on their past and, through God's Word, are discovering unconditional love and forgiveness of our Father.

- **Your gift of £25** could provide a year's worth of Bible reading notes for two young offenders, letting them know they are loved and forgiven by God.
- **Your gift of £50** helps share the news of a loving and forgiving God with four male or female prisoners who feel lost and alone.
- **Your gift of £75** could help answer more requests from chaplains and prisoners to increase the variety of daily Bible reading notes we send as well as providing different Bible-based books and DVDs.

Please fill in the 'Gift to CWR' section on the order form at the back of this publication, completing the Gift Aid declaration if appropriate. Alternatively you can donate online by visiting out website **www.cwr.org.uk/donate**

On behalf of all those wanting to draw closer to God and who are starting their journey of forgiveness in Christ, thank you for your generosity.

Joy is Jesus

FOR READING & MEDITATION – JOHN 15:1-11

'I have told you this so that my joy may be in you and that your joy may be complete.' (v11)

The words of Jesus in today's text highlight the truth that His joy and our joy are not different joys but one and the same. He says, 'my joy may be in you and … your joy may be complete.' His joy and our joy are not alien but allied. And you cannot receive His joy within you without your own joy being made complete. We are made in the inner structure of our beings for the joy of Jesus – His joy completes ours. Speaking of Jesus, Paul says in Colossians 1:16, 'All things were created by him and for him.' This tells us that the signature of Jesus is upon all creation – we were made by Him and for Him. Sometimes I imagine that if we were able to design an instrument that made it possible to look into the human spirit we would see stamped there the words, 'Made by Jesus, for Jesus.'

FURTHER STUDY

Luke 10:21;
John 17:13;
1 Pet. 1:3-9

1. Why can we equate Jesus with joy?

2. With what does Peter equate our joy?

Another wonderful verse in Colossians tells us that our lives are 'hidden with Christ in God' (Col. 3:3). The springs of joy are out of sight – hidden in Him. Someone said of a man who was joyful in the most dire circumstances, 'I don't know where he gets his joy from … it certainly isn't from what is happening around him.' It was hidden in Jesus – out of sight but not out of reach. So let us move away from the idea some Christians hold that joy will be ours only in heaven. We can, and God wants us to, experience exuberance about life as we make our way towards heaven. Joy that is the fruit of the Spirit is a joy that comes from being right with God, from direct and immediate contact with Jesus and His joy. I once asked a group of Sunday school children what Christian joy is. One little boy said, 'Joy is Jesus.' What better definition is there?

My Father and my God, help me day by day to come closer to Jesus for then I will come closer to joy. Show me anything in my life that may be hindering that desired closeness. In Jesus' name I pray. Amen.

Limp in - leap out

FOR READING & MEDITATION - JAMES 1:1-12

'Consider it pure joy, my brothers, whenever you face trials of
many kinds' (v2)

This is possibly one of the most challenging verses in
the entire Bible – however there is an aspect of joy
that is both interesting and important; it helps to protect
our hearts against the entry of problem emotions. Take
jealousy, for instance. Jealousy can quickly find a lodging
place in a heart that has no joy. But as the heart is filled
with joy the problem emotions are diffused. Again, joy
helps to quash any envy that may arise within us. Instead,
our souls long to share the treasures that we ourselves
have found.

Joy also keeps us alert and alive spiritually.
Infection causes most harm to a body debilitated
by despondency because the immune system
has been weakened. The same thing happens in
the realm of the soul. Destructive thoughts and
emotions infuse the soul with ease when there is
no joy and start to degenerate the health of the
soul. Joy, however, gives them no room. It helps
protect and immunises the spirit against such
attack. So joy is not just the bloom of health; it is
the soul's protection also.

FURTHER STUDY

Gen. 26:18;
Isa. 12:1-6

1. What did Isaac need to do?

2. What is the result of salvation?

Every Christian can experience joy flowing through the
soul as a consequence of receiving new life in Jesus. If you
are conscious that you lack this deep abiding joy, then ask
God to help you to clear away any obstacles and allow joy
to flow in and through you today. A sign I once saw outside
a garage in the USA said, 'Limp in – leap out.' That's what
happens to us when we surrender fully to God. We limp
in and leap out. God is not withholding Himself, so know
that you need not withhold yourself. When the two meet,
joy is inevitable.

**Father, forgive me when I go bumping through life on the broken
springs of pleasure when I ought to be journeying in joy. I submit
my life to You today for spiritual repairs. I limp in - please help
me to leap out. Amen.**

A word with a great history

FOR READING & MEDITATION – PHILIPPIANS 4:1-9

'And the peace of God, which transcends all understanding,
will guard your hearts and your minds in Christ Jesus.' (v7)

We move on now to the third fruit of the Spirit – peace. The order is an inspired one: first love because love is pre-eminent, then joy because joy comes as a result of love and then peace, which is the consequence of joy. This sequence is significant. When we love with the love that Jesus puts in our heart by His Spirit then joy and peace follow as natural consequences. 'Peace', said someone, 'is joy grown quiet and assured.' A church leader once compared joy and peace in this way: 'Joy is peace with its hat thrown high in the air and peace is joy with its arms folded in serene assurance.' How beautiful!

FURTHER STUDY

1 Kings 4:20-25; 5:1-5; Isa. 57:18-21

1. What did peace enable Solomon to complete?

2. Contrast those who believe with the wicked.

William Barclay said that the word 'peace' came into the New Testament with a great history. It corresponds to the Hebrew word *shalom*. In classical Greek 'peace' was mainly negative, implying freedom from war or hostilities, but in the New Testament the word gathers up the positive elements conveyed by the word *shalom*. The central meaning is completeness and harmony. 'Peace' occurs 88 times in the New Testament, and it appears in every book except I John. This makes the New Testament a book of peace.

Once again it is important to remember that peace is not something that can be manufactured. We cannot work it up any more than we can create any other fruit of the Spirit. It is divinely infused – a glorious consequence of God's presence in the soul. Jesus knew this kind of peace and He offers the same 'completeness' to every one of His disciples: 'my peace I give you … Do not let your hearts be troubled' (John 14:27). When we remain in Jesus we are given a peace that not only transcends all understanding – but all misunderstanding also.

Father, I am conscious that the peace You desire to give me is a peace that reaches right down to the depths of my being. Help me to open up those depths to You today. In Jesus' name. Amen.

What peace is not

FRI
16 SEP

FOR READING & MEDITATION - 2 THESSALONIANS 3:1-16

'Now may the Lord of peace himself give you peace at all times
and in every way.' (v16)

It might be easier for us to more fully understand the true
character of peace if we seek to explore how it differs
from other states of mind with which, at first glance, it has
a resemblance. First, peace is not passivity. Some people
are abnormally inactive and unreactive by temperament.
They just seem to let the world wash by and take no resolute
attitude to life at all. It is possible to look at someone
with a temperament like this and conclude that they are
demonstrating the fruit of the Spirit. But passivity is as far
removed from peace as chalk is from cheese. One is natural,
the other is the result of the Holy Spirit's work in
the fertile soil of our hearts.

FURTHER STUDY

Num. 6:22-26;
Psa. 37:1-11

Again, peace is not achieved by mental
gymnastics. Today's world is full of 'mind-healers'
who promise that if you attend their seminars
or enrol in their courses they will give you the
poise and self-assurance you always wanted. An
advertisement seen frequently in newspapers says,
'Let us show you how to achieve peace of mind.' The
phrase 'peace of mind' in itself reveals the lack of
depth in the approach. You cannot have genuine
peace of mind until you have peace in the depths
of your spirit. It is impossible to have peace of mind if there
is conflict in your spirit.

1. How are we
to bless one
another?

2. How can we
enjoy great
peace?

The peace that is the fruit of the Spirit brings peace to the
mind because the mind is under the influence of the part
of our being that the Bible calls the 'spirit' – the motivating
centre of our lives. When peace flows there then, and only
then, can a person experience true peace of mind. To tinker
with the mind and leave the depths untouched is just to tinker.

**Father God, please breathe into my spirit right now the deep
serenity and peace that characterise Your own nature so that
all who come close to me will feel Your peace. Amen.**

The best possible peace

FOR READING & MEDITATION - MARK 4:35-41

'A furious squall came up, and the waves broke over the boat ...
Jesus was in the stern, sleeping on a cushion' (vv37-38)

We continue reflecting on the differences between God-given peace and other states of mind sometimes described as 'peace'. Peace is not withdrawal. At recurring intervals in the life of the Christian Church various forms of withdrawal have been practised with a view to discovering inner peace. Early Methodism was almost wrecked by a practise known as 'Stillness'. The idea was to withdraw from all activity and remain 'still' before the Lord. This kind of stillness is not to be confused with the supernatural peace that the Spirit brings to the hearts of God's people. Stillness is something achieved; peace is something given. I his essay 'Sesame and Lillies' John Ruskin wrote, 'He only is advancing in life whose heart is getting softer, whose blood warmer, whose brain quicker, whose spirit is entering into living peace.' Notice the words, 'whose spirit is entering into living peace'. Peace, to be genuine peace, must be a living peace – not the peace of retreat from responsibility. God-given peace is, like joy, entirely independent of circumstances.

FURTHER STUDY

Exod. 14:1-18;
Eph. 2:11-18

1. Why did Moses remain calm when the Israelites panicked?

2. How can we experience peace?

The fact that peace, like joy, is independent of circumstances is brought out most clearly in today's passage. The disciples were in a boat on the Sea of Galilee when a fierce storm descended, causing them to become very afraid. There were 13 storms in the boat that night – one on the lake and 12 in the hearts of the disciples. But where was Jesus? Asleep in the stern of the boat – the worst place to be in a storm apparently. There He was enjoying the best possible peace – sleep. The peace of God does not require easy circumstances in order to operate. Nothing can push it under and nothing can push it over.

Lord Jesus, how I long for the same inner calmness that pervaded Your life when You were here on earth. Help me to let You live Your life more fully in me this day and every day. Amen.

How peace continues

FOR READING & MEDITATION - ISAIAH 26:1-12

'You will keep him in perfect peace, whose mind is stayed on You,
because he trusts in You.' (v3, NKJV)

Yesterday we ended by saying that Jesus enjoyed the best possible peace – sleep – in the worst possible place – the stern of the boat. We see another demonstration of this deep place of peace that Jesus experienced when, as the ugly arms of the cross stretched out to take Him, He said, 'Peace I leave with you; my peace I give you' (John 14:27). Or, as I have heard it put, 'Galilee in storm and Calvary in darkness both set it off.'

The issue we must now face is this: although peace is something given rather than something achieved, its continuance is assured as we follow God's way of living. If, for example, we decide to give in to temptation, we will soon find that peace eludes us. Scripture tells us, 'There is no peace ... for the wicked' (Isa. 57:21). Why? Because we were originally designed to live in a particular way – God's way.

Our text for today gives us another condition on which continuing peace depends: 'You will keep him in perfect peace, whose mind is stayed on You.' Notice the words 'stayed on You'. This highlights that in order to enjoy continuous peace there is to be a conscious centring on God. He is not the place of occasional reference but of continuous reference. Furthermore, He is to be the centre of our trust: 'because he trusts in You'. W.B. Yeats describes, in these gripping lines from his poem 'The Second Coming', the results of a lack of trust in God:

> Things fall apart, the centre cannot hold,
> Mere anarchy is loosed upon the world.

Things really do fall apart when the centre does not hold – and no centre will hold if it is not fixed on God.

FURTHER STUDY

Psa. 119:161-168;
Matt. 11:28-30

1. Who will experience great peace?

2. How can we experience rest?

God, I see that unless I am held at the centre of my being then I am just not held. Hold me at my centre, dear Lord – today and every day. In Jesus' name I ask it. Amen.

Wholehearted faith

FOR READING & MEDITATION - MARK 11:12-26
'"Have faith in God," Jesus answered.' (v22)

Today we look at another scenario on which continuing peace depends – dependent faith in God. A Christian who has wholehearted faith in God will inevitably experience God's perfect peace. If we pretend to believe or only half-believe then this will directly affect our sense of peace.

As followers of Jesus we can have utter faith in the fact that He is God and that He is the Saviour of the world (see Rom. 10:9; Titus 2:13). We can also rest assured that the universe is in the keeping of Infinite Wisdom and Infinite Love, and that God is directing the course of our life (see Psa. 139:16).

FURTHER STUDY

Judg. 6:24-25;
Rom. 5:1-5;
Heb. 4:1-11

1. What is our foundation for perfect peace?

2. Why did the Israelites not enter God's rest?

We can have faith that nothing can happen in the universe without God's permission. And there are no circumstances or situations out of which God cannot bring good (see Rom. 8:28). In the deepest possible sense, we can say with the hymnist Henry F. Lyte:

Whate'er events betide,
Thy will they all perform.

As Christians we can also have wholehearted faith in God being the One who holds the universe together. Colossians 1:16–18 tells us that only God is non-dependent. We are the dependent ones. Humankind may be free, but that freedom is limited and our actions carry consequences. No one can extinguish the stars, pluck the sun from the sky, completely destroy the earth by the use of devastating weaponry, prevent the return of spring or defeat the purposes of God, which are revealed in the Scriptures. God would not allow any of these things to happen for they would be contrary to His design for the universe. The peace of a Christian is therefore established on the rock of reality – the foundation for perfect peace. We can have faith in God, our strong tower and fortress.

Gracious and loving heavenly Father, help me to check on my faith this day and see whether I am really believing or just pretending to believe. I long to be done with all pretence. Lord, increase my faith. Amen.

Utter abandonment

FOR READING & MEDITATION - LUKE 1:26-38

'"I am the Lord's servant," Mary answered. "May it be to me as
you have said."' (v38)

For one more day we reflect on the peace that comes as a result of the Spirit dwelling in our hearts. Those who know the Spirit's perfect peace are those who do not simply resign themselves to God's will but rejoice in the realisation that His will is always best. This attitude is beautifully expressed by Mary, as we have read today.

I once read it summed up in this way: 'To rejoice in God's will suggests mobility – the mobility of a voyager who moves with the motion of the vessel on which he has embarked. It suggests also the abandonment of a servant in attendance on his lord, going only where his master goes. It is the attitude of a child leaving to his mother the care of willing, choosing and acting for him, content to be in her safe and tender keeping.' Streeter and Appasamy, the biographers of the Indian Christian missionary Sadhu Sundar, wrote: 'Realise that to the Sadhu, as to Paul, partnership with Christ was a passion and a privilege that transformed hardship, labour and loss from something which was to be accepted negatively as an unfortunate necessity into something positively welcomed for His sake – and you will understand a little of the secret of the Sadhu's peace.'

FURTHER STUDY

Mark 14:32-42;
Phil. 4:6-7

1. How did Jesus move from distress to peace?

2. How can we do the same?

Jesus, of course, is our supreme example in this. In the words of poet and journalist Robert Nicoll, 'He did not merely accept the will of God when it was brought to Him and laid upon Him. Rather, He went out to meet that loving will and fell upon its neck and kissed it.' Saints down the ages have illustrated through their lives the quality of this perfect peace. Oh, that we, His present-day saints, might show it too.

Father, teach me the art of utter abandonment to Your will. Help me to be like Mary - not just willing, but joyfully willing. This I ask for Your own dear name's sake. Amen.

Pray and let God worry

FOR READING & MEDITATION - LUKE 11:1-13

'one of his disciples said to him, "Lord, teach us to pray"' (v1)

We pause now for a few days from our theme of the fruit of the Spirit, in order to join with many thousands around the world this weekend who are taking part in the National Prayer Weekend. During this month, participants have been receiving prayer requests from family, friends, neighbours and their local communities.

An article was written by a local clergyman who in the United States each Thursday goes to his local coffeeshop, and puts up a sign where he is sitting that reads 'Free Prayer'. The sign also includes a quote from Martin Luther: 'pray, and let God worry'. People stop and pray with him each week. In the article he recounts many of the God-instances and interventions in people's lives in those moments of prayer. He has discovered many pray themselves and would like people to pray for them.

FURTHER STUDY

Matt. 6:5-15

1. Why does Jesus teach people to pray in secret?

2. How is us praying for others doing God's will?

It is at one level a daunting task to offer to pray for others – maybe this is why the disciples asked Jesus to teach them how to pray. As we know, they went on to have remarkable prayer lives, witnessing miracles, praying until rooms shook, even praying for their persecutors, but it began with this simple, reassuring, disarming admission of need. None of us find prayer particularly easy. We all, at times, wonder how best to pray, and why some prayers have an amazing impact, while some seem to have none at all.

Prayer is not a technique. It is powerful because God is powerful. Jesus tells us to address our prayers to 'our Father in heaven' (see Matt. 6:9). In these four words, we see both His love (Father) and His power (in heaven). And, most importantly, prayer is not only powerful but it is also personal.

My Father and my God, like the disciples I ask You teach us to pray. This weekend as we your children pray for others and ourselves, may we not only experience Your power but know You personally. In Jesus' name. Amen.

Together we can
revive a nation!

This weekend (23–25 September 2016) CWR is holding the second National Prayer Weekend.

During this weekend, individuals, groups and churches around the world are joining together to pray for their local communities.

Over the past few weeks, prayer requests from neighbours, colleagues, schools and local businesses have been collected and this coming weekend we will be joining together to pray.

Whether you have already handed out prayer invitations or just found out about the National Prayer Weekend today, you can still participate. We can all pray for those around us this weekend and discover what happens when we cover our nation in prayer, so be sure to join in!

Spread the word and pray with thousands of others around the world for your village, town or city. Visit **www.national-prayer-weekend.com** for more information on how you can get involved.

Let us know how your weekend goes! Connect with us on
Facebook (National Prayer Weekend) or
Twitter (@NPWtogether).

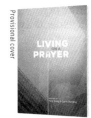

Provisional cover

Living on a Prayer
In support of the National Prayer Weekend, Pete Greig and Carla Harding from the 24-7 Prayer team have written a 16-page easy-to-read booklet introducing everyone to the importance of prayer in our daily lives.
ISBN: 978-1-78259-585-4
£4.99 (Pack of 10)

Prayer is relational

FOR READING & MEDITATION - JOHN 15:1-17

'If you remain in me and my words remain in
you, ask whatever you wish, and it will be given you' (v7)

Yesterday we looked briefly at the idea of prayer for others. Offering to pray for people is not as alien as we might think. Just about everyone prays at some point in their life: arrow type prayers from roadsides to hospital chapels, from football fans during a penalty shoot-out to sighs of thankfulness at the hearing of good news. In fact, surveys tell us that in the UK, 1 in 6 people pray daily and 1 in 5 people believe in the power of prayer. This is at one level unsurprising. But what is interesting is that this is way more than the number of people regularly attending church!

FURTHER STUDY

1 Kings 19:1-18

1. What does this passage teach us about listening for God's voice?

2. How can prayer give us direction?

As we offer to pray for people they sometimes ask why we need to pray since God is *omniscient* (all-knowing) and *omnipotent* (all-powerful). What difference do our prayers really make? Simply speaking, there are at least two really good reasons to pray: firstly, it's *relationship*: prayer is how we re-connect and grow in our relationship with God. Secondly, it's *partnership*: prayer is how we partner our wills with God's will to change the world in which we live. In *The Message*, Eugene Peterson paraphrases Jesus' words in today's reading as this: 'When you're joined with me and I with you, the relation intimate and organic, the harvest is sure to be abundant.' The real power of prayer is rooted in our relationship with Jesus.

Prayer is ultimately a two-way conversation with God in which we speak with Him honestly, sharing our thoughts, thanks and requests, and in which we also listen for His 'still small voice' (1 Kings 19:12, KJV). Good communication is the key to every human relationship, and it is especially vital in our relationship with God.

Gracious God, help me to not only talk constantly with You today as I might talk with a friend, sharing my thoughts, thanks and requests, but that I might also hear Your still small voice. Amen.

Abba Father

FOR READING & MEDITATION - ACTS 4:13-35

'After they prayed, the place where they were meeting was shaken.
And they were all filled with the Holy Spirit' (v31)

We know that Jesus addressed His prayers to 'Abba' – the Aramaic word for 'dad'. As we begin to realise and live in the light of the fact that God loves and likes us, we will learn more and more to feel that when we pray it's not a 'twisting of God's arm', having to persuade Him to answer our prayers.

God loves to be involved in the lives of His children, and to respond to our prayers. 'How much more will your Father in heaven give good gifts to those who ask him' (Matt. 7:11). If you have experienced the care and love of a good father or father figure, be assured your Father in heaven is even better, even kinder, even more forgiving. If you have not known this, or have experience of a father who was distant, absent or cruel, it is such good news that you can know the true love and healing of a heavenly Father.

FURTHER STUDY

John 14:11-27

1. What promises does Jesus give to His followers?

2. How do love and obedience work together?

Some people find it hard to grasp God's love, and others struggle to believe in His holiness and power when their prayers aren't answered. When God seems distant, they conclude that while He may be 'nice', miracles and personal breakthroughs will just not happen. The theological truth is that God is both 'imminent' (close) and 'transcendent' (far beyond our understanding). There is an old Hebrew saying: 'God is not a kindly old uncle. He is an earthquake.' This is good news because there are problems that a kindly old uncle can only smile at, but an earthquake can shift. The apostle Paul says that God can do 'immeasurably more than all we ask or imagine' (Eph. 3:20). In John 14, Jesus says that as we put our trust in Him and step out in faith we will do greater works than Him. That's the confidence that God has in us His children.

Loving Father, today may I not only understand your Father heart in my mind, but give me I pray a new and fresh revelation in my heart and life. Help me today to walk tall as Your child. In the peerless name of Jesus. Amen.

Pray without ceasing

FOR READING & MEDITATION - ROMANS 8:18-27

'We do not know what we ought to pray for, but the Spirit himself
intercedes for us with groans that words cannot express.' (v26)

It is an unspeakable privilege to be able to carry all our
troubles, needs and joys to God in prayer. And, as we do
so, we grow and go deeper in our relationship with Him.
In 1845 an Irish bride sadly drowned the night before her
wedding. Her heartbroken fiancé, a man called Joseph
Scriven, eventually emigrated to Canada. Sometime later
he once again fell in love, but sadly his new fiancé contracted
pneumonia and she too died before their wedding day. After
this double tragedy Joseph Scriven received news that his
mother back in Ireland was seriously ill. In an attempt to
send comfort across the ocean, Joseph wrote a
poem for her titled 'Pray Without Ceasing'. The
words were to become one of the best loved hymns.

**FURTHER
STUDY**

Matt. 11:27-30;
1 Pet. 5:6-11

1. What do these
passages teach
us to do with
our cares and
difficulties?

2. Whenever
we suffer,
what can help
us stand firm
in our faith?

*What a friend we have in Jesus
All our sins and griefs to bear!
What a privilege to carry
Everything to God in prayer.
Oh what peace we often forfeit,
Oh what needless pain we bear,
All because we do not carry
Everything to God in prayer.*

The number one key to prayer is to be yourself.
When a small child scribbles a work of art or words
on a piece of paper and then shows it to their father,
he may not always be able to exactly identify the
word or what the masterpiece is actually of, but will still
proudly put it on display. When we pray either for ourselves
or others we may not know exactly what to pray, but we
can rest in the fact that, as our reading for today reminds
us, our Father in heaven does know, understand and, by His
Spirit, will bring about His good and perfect will in our lives.

**Father God, give me the courage, faith and trust in You to reach
out in prayer today not just for me but for others also. Thank
You that as I pray You are always listening. Amen.**

Good temper

FOR READING & MEDITATION - ECCLESIASTES 7:1-12
'The end of a matter is better than its beginning, and patience
is better than pride.' (v8)

Now we come to the fourth fruit of the Spirit – patience.
The central meaning of this word is 'good temper'. It
denotes a person who does not easily 'fly off the handle'.
  One commentator says, 'This fourth fruit of the Spirit
expresses the attitude to people which never loses patience
with them, however unreasonable they may be, and never
loses hope for them, however unlovely and unteachable
they may be.' Notice the words 'never loses patience with
them'. How many of us, I wonder, could do that without
supernatural help? Archbishop Trench defined the word
'patience' as 'a long holding out of the mind before it
gives room to action or to passion, the self-restraint
which does not hastily retaliate a wrong'. And
Moffatt describes patience as 'the tenacity with
which faith holds out'.
  Good temper must not, however, be confused
with apathy. In the days of the Early Church, a
group called the Stoics made indifference a virtue.
They argued that nothing is worth suffering for, so
taught people to build a wall around their hearts to
keep out all sense of feeling. The early Christians
did not share that view, however, for Christians
care – and because they cared, they suffered. But
through the ministry of the Spirit in their lives they
found poise and good temper amidst their sufferings. Often,
the more we care, the more sensitive we will be to things
that are likely to block our goal of caring, and that is why
patience is so necessary. Once, an evangelist addressing a
meeting was subjected to persistent heckling. Unfortunately
he lost his temper – and also his audience. They saw he had
little to offer except words.

FURTHER STUDY

Num. 20:1-13;
Prov. 16:32

1. What was the result of Moses' impatience?

2. Why may 'successful go getters' not be the best role models?

**Father, help me to become a person of good temper. Please dwell
in me deeply so that I shall be patient and the peaceful exception
amid the disturbed surroundings that I encounter day by day.
Amen.**

Did Jesus lose His temper?

FOR READING & MEDITATION - MARK 3:1-6

'He looked round at them in anger and, deeply distressed at their stubborn hearts, said' (v5)

Yesterday we ended by mentioning the evangelist who lost his temper and also his audience. This leads to the question: Did Jesus ever lose His temper? There are those who think He did and would point to the passage we have read today. I once heard a Christian defend his inability to remain good tempered in all situations in this way: 'If Jesus could not control His temper when faced with the scorn of the Pharisees in Mark 3, and tore them off a strip, then why should I be criticised for my inability to control mine?'

But did the behaviour of Jesus on this occasion result from a loss of temper? I do not believe so. One luminous phrase lights up the story and puts the matter, I feel, in its proper perspective: 'deeply distressed at their stubborn hearts'. Do you see it? The reason why Jesus 'looked round at them in anger' was because He was 'deeply distressed at their stubborn hearts'. The cause of His anger was distress, not loss of temper – distress caused by their insensibility to human need. It was distress caused by what was happening to someone else, not personal pique at what was happening to Him. When we get angry it is most often because our ego has been wounded and hits back, not in redemption, but in retaliation. There is a temper that is redemptive and there is a temper that is retaliatory. The redemptive temper burns with the steady fire of redemptive intention; the retaliatory temper simply burns you up. It is intended to burn the other person up, but all it serves to do is to burn you.

Patience that is the fruit of the Spirit works in us – if we let it – to temper our purposes to kingdom purposes, and to kingdom purposes alone.

FURTHER STUDY

Prov. 19:11; 30:33; John 2:13-17

1. What gives us patience and avoids strife?
2. What is the difference between passion and anger?

My Father and my God, dwell so deeply in me by Your Spirit that my temper shall be tempered and produce no tempests - either in myself or in others. For Jesus' sake I ask it. Amen.

How Jesus handled tension

FOR READING & MEDITATION - LUKE 12:35-53

'But I have a baptism to undergo, and how distressed I am
until it is completed!' (v50)

Our conclusion yesterday was that Jesus' behaviour when He looked round at the Pharisees 'in anger' was not prompted by bad temper but had a redemptive purpose. The motive was not to hurt, but to heal. Far too often when we display anger it is for destructive purposes rather than constructive ones.

Although Jesus was free from bad temper, He was not free from tension. I am using the word 'tension' in the sense of being in a state of moderate stress. A certain amount of tension is a necessary part of life. Indeed, Jesus experienced it, and so will we. Tension is not always a bad thing. For example, the violin or guitar string that is free from tension is incapable of producing music, but when tightened it 'sings' in a way that delights the ear. The tension that Jesus felt was a tension that was harnessed to the interests of others. He was on His way to the cross, and the tension would not end until He pronounced the words, 'It is finished' (John 19:30).

The tension, however, did not leave Jesus frustrated and bad tempered; it left Him calm and composed, with a prayer for the forgiveness of His enemies upon His lips. It drove Him, not to pieces, but to peace – the peace of achievement and victory. This was because the tension was harnessed to God's perfect will – hence it was a constructive urge. Unfortunately, many of our tensions drive us, not towards pursuing God's will, but towards pursuing our own will. We are more concerned for ourselves than for the divine interests. This kind of driving will succeed only in driving us to distraction.

FURTHER STUDY

Neh. 1:1-4;
2:1-6; 6:15-16

1. How did circumstances affect Nehemiah?

2. How did he handle his emotions?

Dear Lord, teach me how to harness my tensions to Your purposes so that they are transformed into rhythm and song. In Jesus' name I ask it. Amen.

'I was saved last night'

FOR READING & MEDITATION - EPHESIANS 5:8-21

'Be filled with the Spirit ... Sing and make music in your heart to the Lord, always giving thanks to God the Father' (vv18-20)

We have talked about how patience can be seen as temper transformed from bad to good. This happens when we allow the Holy Spirit to infuse us with His presence. Today's reading highlights this. When looking at dictionary definitions of the word patience, most talk about the ability to accept delays, problems or suffering without becoming annoyed, anxious or complaining – surely we need the Spirit's help with that! When He is allowed to work in us, He does indeed change our perceptions, providing His understanding, so that we respond to life's situations with praise rather than with pique.

FURTHER STUDY

Matt. 27:11-14, Rom. 12:12

1. Why was the governor amazed?

2. What is the antidote to pressure and affliction?

Here is a great example of the Holy Spirit working in a man's heart: a miner who lived during the Welsh Revival of 1904 was notorious for his bad temper. His job was to look after the pit ponies, and whenever they did anything wrong he would swear and hit out at them with a stick. People learned to keep out of his way, for they knew that he could as easily turn on them. One night he went to a revival meeting, was gloriously converted and wonderfully filled with the Holy Spirit. The next day one of the ponies stepped on his foot. The other miners waited for the explosion – but nothing happened. One man asked, 'Are you sick?' 'No,' he replied. 'Why do you ask?' 'Well,' said the man, 'I know how quickly you get upset about things, and when the pony stepped on your foot and you didn't lose your temper I thought you must be unwell.' 'I'm not unwell,' said the converted miner. 'Last night I went to the revival meeting and God got hold of me and changed me on the inside. Now I don't want to swear, I just want to praise Him in everything.' What a wonderful transformation!

Dear Father, let Your Spirit take His place deep within me so that in the hour of pressure and crisis I shall react to everything in a truly Christian way. In Jesus' name I pray. Amen.

Having the last word

FOR READING & MEDITATION - 1 THESSALONIANS 5:12-24

'And we urge you, brothers, warn those who are idle, encourage the
timid, help the weak, be patient with everyone.' (v14)

Continuing our reflections on the quality of patience, I
would like to share with you the testimony of a woman
called Mary who writes of the great change that took place
in her heart after her conversion.

'I went out to shut the chickens up for the night and found
that the boys had closed the door and turned out the light,
and all the chickens were outside. Chickens can't see in the
dark, and if you shine a light on them, it blinds them. A little
while ago, before my conversion, I would have given the boys
a good spanking and made them get the chickens in. That
night I didn't even stop singing! I went to turn the
light on and found that the bulb had burned out.

**FURTHER
STUDY**

Prov. 15:18;
1 Tim. 6:3-11

Instead of being disgusted, as I would have been BC
(before Christ), I just got a new one, and then I got
those chickens in with such tenderness that I even
surprised myself. When the last chicken was in, I
thanked my Father for helping me get them all in
so easily by controlling, not the chickens, but me.'
What the Spirit did for Mary, He can do for every
single one of us – providing, of course, we have
surrendered our lives to Jesus.

1. What should
we avoid?

2. What should
we pursue?

Another woman, after giving her life to Jesus, found herself
being provoked by her family. She spoke of how, 'I used to
have a violent temper and my family were careful how they
talked to me. It was a goal of mine always to have the last
word. Following my conversion, my family used to test me
by saying all the things they knew used to annoy me. If it
had not been for the presence of the Spirit in my life, I know
I would not have had the patience to handle their remarks.
I still have the last word – but the last word is silence.'

**Father, at those times when the last word needs to be silence,
help me to have that last word. Drive deep into my heart the
thought that I always lose when I lose my temper rather than
exercising patience. Amen.**

'Laughter as a corollary'

FOR READING & MEDITATION - JOB 8:1-22

'He will yet fill your mouth with laughter and your lips with shouts of joy.' (v21)

We spend another day focusing on this fourth fruit of the Spirit – patience. A surprising thing takes place in those who allow the Holy Spirit to infuse them – impatience and bad temper are replaced by a growing sense of humour. God has given us the gift of humour, not only to laugh *at* things, but to laugh *in* the midst of things. I am not suggesting that we ought to use laughter to deny realities, but humour often reduces things to their proper size. I once heard a preacher say, 'There is no good in a movement or a person where there is no good humour, for goodness has laughter as a corollary.'

'Laughter as a corollary' – what a perfect phrase. There is something sadly amiss when a person who, when of course at appropriate times, cannot break out into hearty laughter.

FURTHER STUDY

Prov. 17:22;
Heb. 6:9-15;
James 5:7-11

1. How did Abraham receive God's promises?

2. Why can we be patient with God's timing?

I once heard of a member of a para-military organisation who was wonderfully converted. He spent the first month after his conversion in the home of a minister who said of him, 'It was two weeks before I saw him smile, and when I spoke to him about this he explained, "I have been in a grim business, plotting against people – and the way I was living, there was just no reason to smile, let alone laugh."' How tragic – 'just no reason to smile'. If, on appropriate occasions, you feel you cannot smile or laugh, why not ask God to help you receive His wonderful sense of humour.

Over the years I have watched countless groups come for training in Christian Counselling. Many arrive burdened with fear, guilt and apprehension. We invite them to share their fears and get them out into the open. They do. Then the laughter begins. The laughter gets heartier as the week goes on. By the end of the training they feel much lighter.

God my Father, I am so thankful that goodness has laughter as a corollary. Help me, I pray, to experience a lightness and security of soul that enables me to laugh when appropriate, even at myself. In Jesus' name. Amen.

Warm goodwill to others

FOR READING & MEDITATION - COLOSSIANS 3:1-15

'As God's chosen people ... clothe yourselves with compassion, kindness, humility, gentleness and patience.' (v12)

The fifth fruit of the Spirit listed in Galatians 5:22 is kindness. 'Kindness' is a very beautiful word; it means 'a kindly disposition, or warm goodwill towards others'. To speak, for example, of an 'unkind Christian' is almost a contradiction in terms. There is some evidence that in the early centuries of the Church, non-Christians used the words 'kindly' and 'Christian' as synonyms. One of the Early Church Fathers (Tertullian, I believe) said, 'The words were so allied in meaning that no harm was done by the confusion.' *The Message* describes kindness as 'a sense of compassion in the heart'. Mother Teresa once gave this instruction, which reflects that meaning nicely: 'Be the living expression of God's kindness ... give ... not only your care, but also your heart.'

I once asked a church youth group which fruit of the Spirit they would be willing to do without if they had to settle for eight instead of nine. Surprisingly, almost everyone in the group said 'kindness'. When I asked why, they explained that for them the word conjured up sentimentality. One person said, 'It makes me think of my kind old aunt. She's a lovely person really but a little gullible, sentimental and easily taken in.' The group had a distorted picture of kindness because it is a misconception to equate a kindly disposition with maudlin sentimentality.

So let's be quite clear what we are talking about when we use the word 'kindness'. It is a God-given virtue endowed by the Holy Spirit that infuses our whole personality and engenders us a sense of compassion towards others. It's there inside us; all we have to do is let it flow out.

FURTHER STUDY

Acts 27:42-28:2;
Eph. 2:1-9

1. What was unusual about the islanders?

2. How has God expressed kindness to you?

Gracious Father, help me today to be clothed with kindness. Make me a person who can show warmth and goodwill to others. I ask this for Your own dear name's sake. Amen.

What it means
to be a pilgrim

Peter Morden (author of *John Bunyan: The People's Pilgrim*) has worked with co-author Ruth Broomhall to create a 40-day devotional based on Bunyan's *The Pilgrim's Progress* – helping readers grasp for themselves what it means to be a pilgrim, walking every day with God.

Here, Peter and Ruth tell us more about their new book *To Be a Pilgrim* ...

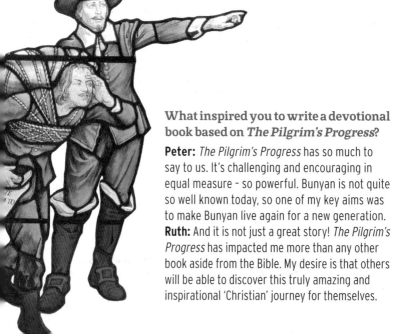

What inspired you to write a devotional book based on *The Pilgrim's Progress*?

Peter: *The Pilgrim's Progress* has so much to say to us. It's challenging and encouraging in equal measure – so powerful. Bunyan is not quite so well known today, so one of my key aims was to make Bunyan live again for a new generation.

Ruth: And it is not just a great story! *The Pilgrim's Progress* has impacted me more than any other book aside from the Bible. My desire is that others will be able to discover this truly amazing and inspirational 'Christian' journey for themselves.

Why is *The Pilgrim's Progress* important and relevant today?

Peter: The lessons Bunyan teaches us are certainly relevant for the twenty-first century; in fact, they're relevant for every age.

Ruth: In over 25 years of engaging with the book, as teacher, youth and children's leader, student and writer, I have found that *The Pilgrim's Progress* never fails to enthuse and inspire children and adults alike.

What do you most hope people will get from *To Be a Pilgrim*?

Ruth: Bunyan's hope was for burdened readers to experience real freedom in Christ, be strengthened in their own Christian lives and challenged to share their faith with others.

Peter: I agree! *The Pilgrim's Progress* has so much to teach us about what it means to follow Jesus. It helps us cope with suffering, persevere on the journey of discipleship, grow in holiness, and share our faith with others. We want to make these, and other encouraging lessons, accessible for as many people as possible, as Bunyan would have wanted.

To discover more about *To Be a Pilgrim* visit **www.cwr.org.uk/store** or see the back of these notes. If you'd like to find out more about the remarkable life of John Bunyan, Peter Morden's book *John Bunyan: The People's Pilgrim* as well as new companion DVD are also available.

A debased word

FOR READING & MEDITATION - EPHESIANS 4:17-32

'Be kind and compassionate to one another, forgiving each other,
just as in Christ God forgave you.' (v32)

Yesterday we said that some people have the wrong idea of kindness and view it as just maudlin sentimentality. It is surprising how devalued the word 'kindness' has become in both Christian and non-Christian thought.

Most Christians accept the merit of kindness because it is spoken of in Scripture but have no real desire to acquire the virtue because, to them, it conjures up images of softness and weakness. The world uses the word 'kindness', but separated from any thought of God, kindness becomes a mild compensation for a lack of firmness and clear thinking.

FURTHER STUDY

2 Sam. 9:1-13;
Titus 3:1-7

1. How did David show kindness?

2. What did God make apparent?

People say, rather patronisingly in some cases, 'Oh, he's a kind person' – and they leave it there. Since the word has worn rather thin in the currency of the world (and in some parts of the Church) there is a great need to see it minted afresh and gleaming bright in the commerce of modern-day Christian life.

Think with me a little more about what kindness, the fruit of the Spirit, is not. Kindness is not being a 'do-gooder'. In fact, the word in the original Greek does not imply active goodness but a disposition of goodwill, although active goodness may be one expression of it. Many think that kindness is demonstrated by giving money to people who have a financial need. But giving money to people who appear to need it without being guided by the Spirit can cause complications and difficulties. Giving to people at the wrong time can also take from them something of greater value than what is being given. Though this may be a slight aside, it is worth saying, I think, that there are few matters in which we have more need of the Holy Spirit's direction than in the matter of our giving.

Father, I want my kindness to be genuine kindness - the sort of kindness that helps people and does not hamper them. Help me to be open to Your Holy Spirit cultivating more of this fruit in me. Amen.

'Your Father in heaven ... causes his sun to rise on the evil and the good, and sends rain on the righteous and the unrighteous.' (v45)

Now that we have considered what kindness is not we start to focus on what it does involve. It is of great significance that in the Bible the word 'kindness' is used most frequently in relation to God. I have noted William Barclay as saying, 'It is something of a joyous revelation to discover that when the King James Version calls God "good", again and again the meaning is not just moral goodness but kindness.'

The goodness of God is not something we need shrink away from in fear; rather it is something that draws us to Him with cords of love. This does not mean, of course, that God is indifferent to our inherently rebellious nature. On the contrary, His goodness is what led Him to provide through the cross a way whereby our sin can be forgiven and forgotten.

The beautiful term 'loving kindness' is used in certain books of the Old Testament in some of the older translations of the Bible, especially in the Psalms. In the New Testament, however, we have the supreme expression of kindness – the death of Jesus for us – which has made the addition of the word 'loving' unnecessary. And it is clear that Jesus' great sacrifice has a bearing on our own behaviour. Take Paul's instruction to the Philippians, for example: 'Your attitude should be the same as that of Christ Jesus' (Phil. 2:5). We are to not merely do as Jesus did but have been invited to receive and share in the same attitude as He did. This shows that kindness involves more than just actions but attitudes as well. I can think of no better definition of kindness than this: kindness is treating others in the same way that God has treated us.

FURTHER STUDY

Jer. 31:3-9;
Eph. 4:32-5:2

1. How are love and kindness linked?

2. Why should we be kind to one another?

Father, just as You let Your kindly rain fall on the evil and the good, help me to rain kindness on everyone I meet today regardless of who or what they are. In Jesus' name. Amen.

'What this sad world needs'

FOR READING & MEDITATION - PROVERBS 19:20-29
'What a man desires is unfailing love' (v22)

Now that we have discovered that true kindness is to have
the same attitude as Jesus Christ – 'Your attitude should
be the same as that of Christ Jesus' (Phil. 2:5) – we must
consider how to develop and grow in kindness. The poetess
Ella Wheeler Wilcox says in her poem 'The World's Need':

So many gods, so many creeds,
So many paths that wind and wind,
When all that this sad world needs,
Is just the art of being kind.

**FURTHER
STUDY**

Mark 14:3-9;
2 Pet. 1:3-8

1. How can
kindness linger
in the memory?

2. What should
we add to
our faith?

Human kindness may be important, but God-
infused kindness is even more important. It is,
indeed, what 'this sad world needs'.
The importance of kindness is seen by the fact
that an act of kindness lingers on in the memory.
Once, I was due to speak to a large audience at
the Colston Hall, Bristol, but was feeling a little
weighed down by personal circumstances. Just as
I was about to step onto the platform a few ladies
who represented an organisation called 'Women
Aglow' handed me a little box in which was a
beautiful flower. With it was a message: 'We love
you and are praying for you.' That kindness, and the spirit
that prompted it, was like a star on a dark night. I have never
forgotten it and I never will forget it.
If kindness can minister such comfort and encouragement
then how imperative it is that we ask God to ripen this
fruit within us. Of the many things associated with Paul's
shipwreck on Malta, Luke recalls in particular that the
'islanders showed us unusual kindness' (Acts 28:2). Pause
for a moment – is there someone you could encourage today
with a simple act of kindness?

**Father, help me to demonstrate Your fruit of kindness this day
so that somebody, somewhere, may use it as a light to lighten
their darkness. In Jesus' name I ask this. Amen.**

Can't help being kind

FOR READING & MEDITATION – MATTHEW 25:31-46

'The King will reply, "I tell you the truth, whatever you did for one of
the least of these … you did for me."' (v40)

Kindness, as today's text shows, is revealed in acts of
generosity and compassion done out of a desire to
please Jesus. The more we abide in Him and base our lives
on His teaching, placing ourselves in His presence, the
more kindness will grow in us. Once again I return to this:
kindness that comes from the Spirit is not the result of trying
to be kind but flows from us because of our relationship
with Jesus Christ. As we abide in Jesus the fruit grows and
ripens of its own accord.

Interestingly, the kindest Christians are those who have
no ambition to be kind. This is not to say that
they do not desire to be kind, but they do not try
to manufacture their kindness. Motivated with
a longing to be more like Jesus every day, their
thoughts are not on their personal reputation but
on how they reflect Jesus. Such people come across
as clearly self-forgetful, so much so that what
was said of Anglican cleric and social reformer
Samuel Barnett can be said of them also: 'He forgot
himself even to the extent of forgetting that he
had forgotten!'

A real danger of the Christian life is that we may
actually become selfish in our consuming longing
to be unselfish. Only as our roots go down daily
into God and His Son Jesus, through prayer and
meditation on His Word, can we be kept secure from the
temptation to focus on growth for its own sake rather than
for His sake. The person whose kindness is motivated by a
desire for praise gives up when the praise is not forthcoming.
Christians whose kindness flows from their relationship
with God never give up. They just can't help being kind.

**FURTHER
STUDY**

Matt. 15:29-39;
Acts 11:27-30

1. What
motivated
Jesus' act of
kindness?

2. How did the
early Christians
follow Jesus'
example?

**Father God, help me to spend time with You so that in the legislature
of my heart You may write the law of kindness. Help me to come
under its sway forever. Amen.**

The essential flavouring

FOR READING & MEDITATION – 2 CORINTHIANS 6:1-13

'As servants of God we commend ourselves in every way …
in purity, understanding, patience and kindness' (vv4,6)

One final thought concerning kindness needs to engage our attention before we move: nothing else we do can atone for a lack of kindness. Many people excuse themselves for a lack of kindness by pointing to the things they do for someone. For instance, they may argue, 'I'm working my fingers to the bone for him.' Yes, but fleshless fingers will not atone for unkind words and attitudes.

Ministers or church workers who work hard but lack this essential gift of kindness are no exception. Paul lists over 25 things in the passage we have read that are marks of a true servant of God, and notice how he puts kindness right in the middle of them. At the centre of all his 'proofs' is kindness. I do not think it is by chance that kindness is also the middle virtue of the nine fruits of the Spirit. Without kindness there is no virtue in the other virtues. This one puts flavour in all the rest; without it they are insipid and tasteless. So to grow in kindness is to grow in virtues that are flavoured with a certain spirit – the Spirit of Jesus.

FURTHER STUDY

Jer. 9:23-24;
Luke 6:27-38

1. In what does God delight?

2. How does God respond to the ungrateful and wicked?

It remains a fact, however, that although the Holy Spirit indwells Christians, sadly there are those who are not kind. Some well-known Christian leaders have not been as distinguished in this fruit of the Spirit as in others, and have worn their halo a little askew. A number are stern and unfeeling. They are harsh with words. Disciplined as they are in virtue, they have become censorious and critical, and their passion for righteousness makes it hard for them to show tenderness to those who do not yet know Jesus. Unlike any of us, Jesus upheld God's laws completely – yet He was called the 'friend of … sinners' (Matt. 11:19).

My Father and my God, although I never want to lessen the gravity of sin, I long to be a person who shows tenderness to those who are enmeshed in it. Help me become that type of person. In Jesus' name. Amen.

FOR READING & MEDITATION – ACTS 10:34-48

'God anointed Jesus of Nazareth with the Holy Spirit and power,
and ... he went around doing good and healing' (v38)

We come now to the sixth fruit of the Spirit – goodness. Most commentators agree that it is the hardest fruit to define as the word 'good' is used so widely that it can mean almost everything and nearly nothing. In some circles, for example, a person is regarded as good if they simply keep out of the hands of the police whereas in other circles goodness consists of being a highly respectable person. *The Message* refers to goodness as a 'conviction that a basic holiness permeates things and people'.

It is the view of most writers and Bible commentators that God-cultivated goodness is not just a matter of doing good things (though it includes that) but that it is essential goodness. Edwin Chaplin, a Christian writer, put it well when he said, 'Goodness consists not just in the outward things we do but in the inward thing we are.' Goodness, like kindness, has first to be an attitude before it becomes an action. In fact, some commentators believe it is more non-verbal than verbal – it is evidenced not so much in words as in one's whole demeanour. And it is a goodness that unconsciously proclaims itself. Those who possess it have a certain presence about them. It is radiated so powerfully that it is doubtful whether anyone could be near to it and yet be unaware of it. Many people, especially non-Christians, might not be able to describe what they feel in the presence of this goodness, but they do feel something nevertheless. And that something is the character of Jesus flowing in and through one of His followers.

How wonderful it is to meet a Christian and feel Jesus coming through, even when that person does not use words. It is Christlikeness at its best.

FURTHER STUDY

Psa. 119:65-68;
Eph. 5:3-10

1. How does God's character relate to what He does?

2. How do we live as children of light?

Father, how I long to be the channel and not the stopping place of all Your blessings to me. Let this grace, as well as the others, be seen in me. In Jesus' name I pray. Amen.

'Secret death'

FOR READING & MEDITATION - ROMANS 6:1-14
'Anyone who has died has been freed from sin.' (v7)

Yesterday we said that the goodness that is the fruit of the Spirit is essential goodness – goodness in the inner parts. In my view, the best summary of the true nature of this sixth fruit is, 'Goodness is the impression a Christian makes as he or she moves on their way, blissfully unaware of the fact that in their demeanour they remind people of Jesus Christ.' Perhaps we can get no nearer to a definition of God-given goodness than that: reminding people of Jesus. But notice the words 'blissfully unaware'. Christians are largely unconscious of this fruit at work within them, for it is not something they try to manufacture but something that flows out of their deep relationship with Jesus.

FURTHER STUDY

Psa. 145:1-21

1. What will God's people celebrate?

2. How does God's goodness relate to all His other qualities?

George Muller of Bristol, who cared for so many orphans in the nineteenth century, was said to demonstrate the fruit of goodness to a remarkable degree. One day George Muller was urged to share what he considered to be the power behind his ministry. He surprised his questioner by talking about his 'secret death'. 'There was a day', he said, 'when I died; utterly died.' As he spoke, he bent lower until he almost touched the floor. Then he continued, 'I died to George Muller, his opinions, preferences, tastes and will; died to the world, its approval or censure; died to the approval or blame even of my brethren and friends; and since then I have studied only to show myself approved of God.'

In those who manifest the fruit of goodness, one thing is always clear: they have died to their own interests and have returned to live for the interests of Christ.

Gracious and loving Father, help me also to die to my own interests so that I might live for Your interests. Please do whatever is necessary to bring me to this point - today. In Jesus' name I ask it. Amen.

Death of the ego

FOR READING & MEDITATION - GALATIANS 2:11-21

'I have been crucified with Christ and I no longer live,
but Christ lives in me.' (v20)

Yesterday we mentioned George Muller, who talked about his 'secret death'. Here in today's reading the apostle Paul also talks about a 'death', but obviously one that he had no intention of keeping secret.

In the main, there are two differing views on this passage. One view is that Paul is referring here to the teaching he expounded in Romans 6, namely that when Jesus died at Calvary we all 'died' with Him, but because He came back from the dead we now apply ourselves to appropriating that resurrection power and allow it to work in us to overcome self and sin. Paul's statement about being 'crucified with Christ', it is claimed, has reference to that. Others take the view that Paul is referring to a specific experience in his life following his conversion when his 'old self' (the carnal nature) 'died' to self-interest. With the 'old self' crucified, the self in which Jesus lives rises in its stead.

Personally, I see truth in both these views. Sanctification is a process but it can also take place at a particular point in time. Many Christians testify, as did George Muller, that even though they were applying the sanctifying power of the Holy Spirit in their lives day by day, there came a moment or a period when they experienced a critical putting to death of their ego. Not everyone, it seems, is brought by the Spirit to experience sanctification at a particular time, but it is significant that many of the saints whose lives are marked by a high degree of holiness testify to such an experience. Let your heart be open to God on this matter today and listen to what He might say to you. Perhaps this could be the day on which your ego dies.

FURTHER STUDY

Gal. 5:13-26;
1 Pet. 2:24-25

1. How can we be both dead and alive at the same time?

2. What has happened to our passion and desires?

My Father and my God, I choose what You choose. If today You choose to lead me into a deeper understanding of how to die to my self-interest then I choose to follow. Guide me, my Father. In Jesus' name. Amen.

'Pharisaism in overalls'

FOR READING & MEDITATION - LUKE 18:9-14

'The Pharisee stood up and prayed about himself:
"God, I thank you that I am not like other men"' (v11)

Perhaps you are wondering why I keep repeating the fact that the different aspects of the fruit of the Spirit are not achieved through self-effort. I feel compelled to make this point again and again because over the years I have come across large numbers of Christians who believe the fruit of the Spirit is produced by their own human effort rather than by depending on the Holy Spirit. So many Christians equate the fruit of the Spirit with fulfilling the demands of an ethical code that it is important to make it absolutely clear that these fruits are produced not by us living up to a standard. Rather we let God work in our hearts so that the fruit can grow and then flow out from ourselves to others – in other words, fruit is produced through the activity of the Holy Spirit.

FURTHER STUDY

Luke 15:22-30;
Phil. 3:1-11

1. How was the older son moral but fruitless?

2. What did Paul reject and what did he embrace?

If ethical mastery is gained by self-effort alone then the person who attains it comes to have pride in their achievement and falls prey to Pharisaism – pride in one's own moral achievements. Those who keep the ethical code by self-effort often have a taut will and, though they might not realise it, they lapse into the sin of independence – depending on self rather than the Spirit. People who struggle to exude goodness at times appear stern and rigid and seem to regard themselves as being moral athletes. Someone has called this type of attitude 'Pharisaism in overalls', in other words, working hard at being moral instead of allowing Jesus' life to flow through.

Those whose goodness is not imposed but exposed by their deep relationship with the Lord are fully human and exude the character of Christ. The kingdom of God belongs to such as these.

Father, I see that if I strut through life in an attitude of arrogance and pride I soon stumble. But when I surrender, I succeed. Help me to remember this – today and every day. Amen.

The disease of self-interest

FOR READING & MEDITATION – ROMANS 15:14-22

'I myself am convinced … that you yourselves are full of goodness … competent to instruct one another.' (v14)

Because the blight of self-interest is so difficult to recognise, it might be helpful to focus on examples of ordinary things done or said by people that are, nevertheless, indicative of the ease with which we slip into self-interest.

A man whose mother died just as he was due to go on holiday and who was therefore obliged to stay at home until the funeral was overheard saying to the minister who tried to comfort him, 'I will miss my mother greatly … but I've lost nearly half my holiday.'

I remember that just after my wife's death a man came up to me and said, 'How is your wife?' Before I had time to reply and explain that she had gone to be with the Lord he launched into a five-minute discourse on how his wife had been up all night with toothache. There was nothing wrong in him wanting to tell me about his wife's toothache but the problem was that he did not wait for me to answer the question he put to me: 'How is your wife?' Self-interest? Perhaps so.

Today's text shows that the Christians in the church at Rome were demonstrating the fruit of goodness in ways that caused the apostle Paul to commend them for their surrender to the Holy Spirit. They were not trying hard to overcome self-interest but were allowing the Spirit to work through them. Notice too that when goodness reigns in a human life it will reveal itself not only in the things we say but also in the things we do. The Christians in Rome were using their knowledge to instruct one another. I once read that 'goodness is not goodness unless it wishes the good of others'. And I would add: not only wishes it but is alert to every opportunity to put goodness into action.

FURTHER STUDY

John 12:1-6;
Acts 9:36-41

1. Why did Judas express an interest in the poor?

2. How did Dorcas express an interest in the poor?

Lord God, so fill my heart, I pray, with Your goodness that it will constantly flow out of me. And may my good intentions always be turned into good actions. This I ask in and through the precious name of Jesus. Amen.

'Her first thought'

FOR READING & MEDITATION – 1 PETER 3:18-4:8

'Therefore, since Christ suffered in his body, arm yourselves also with the same attitude' (4:1)

So often in life our first thought is for ourselves. Generally speaking, we are extremely self-centred – everything has an immediate self-reference. And so deeply ingrained is our self-preoccupation that we ourselves cannot get rid of it. Yet thankfully, through the work of the Holy Spirit in their lives, there are multitudes whose first thoughts are not for themselves but for Jesus and for others. How has this happened? It has happened because the fruit of the Spirit has been growing in their lives – especially the fruit of goodness.

FURTHER STUDY

2 Kings 6:24-25; 7:1-11; Phil. 2:1-8

1. What did the lepers realise?

2. What should we look to?

Take, for example, Catherine Booth, the wife of William Booth, founder of the Salvation Army. When she first learned the deadly nature of the disease that was to kill her slowly through two years of great pain, she allegedly knelt at the side of her husband and said, 'Do you know what was my first thought? That I should not be there to nurse you at your last hour.' Her first thought!

A minister I once visited who had been struck down with polio anxiously asked me, 'But who will care for my people?' It was not of himself he was thinking, but of others.

The self-forgetfulness of both Catherine Booth and the minister who was forced to relinquish his duties because of ill health was not something that was manufactured but something that had been cultivated in them by the indwelling of the Holy Spirit. Their selflessness can be explained in only one way: they had died to themselves. The centre of their lives had shifted from self to Christ and thus the fruit of goodness had ripened in their lives in much the same way as fruit appears in an orchard.

Father, dwell so deeply in me by Your Holy Spirit that I will be lifted out of myself. I would die to myself and live for You – now and for ever. Amen.

Surrendering to goodness

FOR READING & MEDITATION - PHILIPPIANS 2:12-18

'Children of God without fault in a crooked and depraved generation, in which you shine like stars in the universe' (v15)

Although, as we have been saying, goodness is a fruit that can be quite difficult to define, we come close to understanding its true meaning when we think of it in terms of essential goodness – goodness in the inner parts. It is not something that is imposed from without but something that is exposed; it moves not from without to within, but from within to without. Goodness is not self-achievement but Other-achievement – the 'Other' being the Holy Spirit. This God-infused goodness is pure goodness – a goodness that unconsciously proclaims itself.

Christians in whom 'goodness' is growing will not 'use' others but will love them for themselves alone. They will not mentally fit people into their schemes for they have no schemes. Although it is true that the essence of goodness is to be found to some degree in all Christians, in those who have known what it is to die to self it overflows. John Wallace, a Scotsman and the principal of the college where I received my training for the ministry, used to explain in his Scottish accent, 'Goodness, the fruit of the Spirit, is more "felt" than "telt" ... it is not so much actions as attitudes, not so much talking as walking.' God comes close to people in different ways – sinners as well as those who are saved – and one of the methods He frequently uses to call to individuals is through the life of someone in whom the fruit of goodness is ripe.

So, when wanting this fruit of the Spirit to be produced more abundantly in your life – a desire that ought to consume all those who long to be more like Jesus – keep in mind that it reveals itself not when we strain to be good but when we surrender to goodness.

FURTHER STUDY

Rom. 12:9-21

1. What does goodness look like?

2. How can we overcome evil?

Father God, I see that goodness is not something that needs to be grafted on to my life; it is something that grows from within. Teach me how to stop struggling and start surrendering. In Jesus' name. Amen.

The ultimate test of character

FOR READING & MEDITATION - PSALM 51:1-19

'Surely you desire truth in the inner parts' (v6)

Now we start to examine the seventh fruit of the Spirit – faithfulness. Faithfulness is the quality of reliability, trustworthiness or loyal commitment that not only relates to God but makes a Christian someone on whom others can utterly rely and whose word they can utterly accept.

It has been said that the ultimate test of a person's character is: Are there any circumstances in which that person will lie? A Christian worker known to me puts in many hours of service and is prepared to come to the aid of anyone in need, but sadly he cannot always be relied upon to speak the truth. That lack of honesty cancels out much of the value of his accomplishments.

FURTHER STUDY

1 Sam. 16:1-13;
Eph. 4:20-25

1. How does God assess us?

2. What are we to put off and put on?

In a certain Third World country church leaders are obliged to fill out a tax return for their church and to declare its assets. One church owned a valuable gold cross. So that they would not have to pay a large amount of tax, the leaders decided to devalue the cross on the tax return and value it at only a fraction of its real worth. One day the cross was stolen and broken up into small pieces. When the police eventually recovered the pieces, the church leaders went to court to prove the pieces belonged to them. The judge called for a valuation of the gold, and when he was told it was of very high value he declared that the cross could not belong to the church as the stolen cross was of much higher value than the one listed on the church's tax return. So the gold was confiscated by the police. The church leaders remained silent on the issue and did not confess to their falsehood. I am sad to say by so doing they lost not only a cross, they also lost their good character.

Father, help me see even more clearly that unless I live in the truth and by the truth, I dishonour You. May I be faithful to You in all things, dear Lord. For Your name's sake. Amen.

Faithful with the little

FOR READING & MEDITATION - LUKE 16:1-13

'So if you have not been trustworthy in handling worldly wealth,
who will trust you with true riches?' (v11)

We must not think that because faithfulness is listed among the last three qualities on Paul's list it is of lesser importance. So important is it that Jesus says in our reading today, 'He who is faithful in what is least is faithful also in much; and he who is unjust in what is least is unjust also in much' (v10, NKJV).

Over the years, when I see a young man or woman on fire for God, I have often said to myself, 'There goes a young person who will make great strides in the kingdom.' But sadly time and time again I have seen them fail in their faithful fulfilment of small obligations. And then I have said to myself, 'Unless there are great changes, that person will end up like the children of Israel in the wilderness – going around in circles.'

Look again at what Jesus said in our text for today, this time in the New American Standard Bible: 'Therefore if you have not been faithful in the use of unrighteous wealth, who will entrust the true riches to you?' Here the basic principles are laid down. If you are not faithful with the small things, you will not be faithful with the big things. If you are not faithful with the material how can you expect to be entrusted with the spiritual?

FURTHER STUDY

Prov. 8:6-21;
Zech. 4:8-10

1. What are true riches?

2. Why might we despise small things?

But Jesus says one more thing: 'And if you have not been trustworthy with someone else's property, who will give you property of your own? ?' (v12). It's a sobering fact, but nevertheless true, that often those who are not faithful with other people's possessions finish up with nothing of their own. I suggest that we reflect each day on whether we are being faithful with what we have been given. When we are, we will see how God loves to entrust us with more.

Father, I am conscious that day by day You let me be tested with a little. Please help me to be faithful with that so that I can be trusted to handle a lot. In Jesus' name I ask it. Amen.

'Lies have short legs'

'There is nothing concealed that will not be disclosed, or hidden that will not be made known.' (v2)

Both the universe and we ourselves have been created for truth and honesty, and both the universe and we ourselves are alien to untruth and dishonesty. The universe has been made for the same thing as we have been, namely righteousness. Not only the face of God but the face of the universe is set against those who do not live according to His design. Though I know this may sound somewhat hollow in an age that appears rife with dishonesty and corruption, I stand by it nevertheless. The universe has not been created for the success of dishonesty and corruption. A lie breaks itself upon the moral universe – perhaps not today, not tomorrow, but certainly at some point in the future.

FURTHER STUDY

Psa. 78:9-11;
Matt. 27:3-10

1. Why was Ephraim unfaithful?

2. How did Judas' own unfaithfulness break him?

The Tamils of South India have a saying: 'The life of the cleverest lie is only eight days.' I once heard another saying: 'Lies have short legs.' During World War II some altered that saying to 'Lies have one leg' because Goebbels, the German propaganda minister, had one leg that was shorter than the other. A passionate antagonist of Communism is reported to have claimed, 'In our fight against Communism we are handicapped by our decency and honesty.' Since when was honesty and decency a handicap? It is indecency and dishonesty that are handicaps; they bring us into bondage – inwardly and outwardly.

Governments, organisations and institutions that practise dishonesty will be broken from within. History has proved that. The Roman Empire was destroyed not from without, but from within – broken upon the rock of its own corruption. Believe me, no one gets away with anything in a moral universe. No one.

Gracious Father, I see that dishonesty does not belong in Your universe. Please flow into me through Your Holy Spirit so that truth and righteousness will flow out of me every day and everywhere. In Jesus' name. Amen.

The cement of society

FOR READING & MEDITATION - MATTHEW 5:13-20

'You are the salt of the earth. But if the salt loses its saltiness,
how can it be made salty again?' (v13)

One thing is becoming crystal clear as we continue
meditating on faithfulness: there are *always*
consequences to our actions – and that includes dishonesty.
The whole history of humanity endorses this. Do you
remember the first lie uttered by Satan: 'You will not
surely die' (Gen. 3:4)? He keeps on repeating that well-
worn but discredited lie to every member of the human
race. Something dies in us the moment we are dishonest
– not least our self-respect. Lies eat away at our hearts the
moment dishonesty is let in. We are not so much punished
for our sin as by our sin.

I remember once coming across this point: 'There
are two major principles for getting and keeping
political power: (1) let nothing, least of all truth and
honour, interfere with success; (2) be honest and
trustworthy in the little things, but boldly dishonest
in the large ones.' What would be the result of a
person gaining political power by following those
two principles? I will tell you. Like blind Samson,
they would pull down the pillars of society around
their heads and the heads of others also. It is the
ten righteous men who spare the Sodoms of this
world (see Gen. 18:32). Fidelity is the cement that
holds society together; take it away and society implodes,
destroying itself.

It may be stretching the imagination too far by saying
this, but in my opinion the Christian presence, especially
as it represents faithfulness, holds the world on its course.
Civilisation would have disintegrated long ago were it not
for the moral and Christian character that flows out of the
Church into the world. And the more it flows the better –
from each one of us.

**FURTHER
STUDY**

Lev. 19:35-36;
Deut. 25:13-16;
Acts 15:36-40

1. What does the
Lord detest?

2. Why did
Paul not
want to take
John Mark?

**Father, help me to be one who holds the world together by my
character. And let the hallmark of my character be faithfulness
to truth and righteousness. In Jesus' name I ask it. Amen.**

The eight points of testing

FOR READING & MEDITATION - 2 CORINTHIANS 2:12-3:6
'But thanks be to God, who always leads us in triumphal
procession in Christ' (v14)

Already we have looked at three characteristics of the fruit of the Spirit that Paul terms 'faithfulness' – honesty, reliability and a deep concern for truth. A further characteristic is the willingness to carry through on all God's commands to us – keeping faith to the end, which is what Peterson describes as 'loyal commitment' in *The Message*. To help us come through the periods of testing everyone has to face at some time, the Holy Spirit gives us the ability to see things through to the end.

One Christian writer has listed what he believes to be the eight fiercest tests a believer has to face in this world. First, humiliation – a savage and plausible attack on our reputation. Second, suffering – physical, mental or spiritual. Third, bereavement – especially the death of a loved one whose passing was 'untimely'. Fourth, estrangement or treachery from one's family and friends. Fifth, doubt – deep, dark and awful. Sixth, failure – the breaking up of one's life work. Seventh, dereliction – the sense of being forsaken by God. Eighth, a slow, painful and unillumined death.

Not all of us encounter all of these trials, but meeting any one of them can be a strong and severe test. How does a Christian remain faithful in the midst of such fierce circumstances as those listed above? Any overcoming we experience at such times is through the strength of the Holy Spirit. He dwells in us not just for the pleasure of inhabiting our beings, but to enable us to walk through life's struggles. Perhaps you are facing one or more of these eight points of testing this very moment. Then take courage – invite Him in and allow Him to carry you through today.

FURTHER STUDY

John 6:60-69;
1 Tim. 6:11-14

1. Contrast Peter's response with that of other disciples.

2. What should Christians fight?

Father, I am grateful that Your Spirit dwells within me to lead me through life. Even in my darkest trials You are there, inspiring me and helping me to stay faithful in all things. Thank You, Father. Amen.

NEXT ISSUE

A New Perspective

Have you ever wondered why some Christians are suffering and struggling whilst those of seemingly no faith seem to 'sail through life' untouched and unscathed?

In this issue, Selwyn takes us on a journey through Psalm 73, where the psalmist wrestles with and resolves questions of doubt and confusion.

Starting from a place where he is slipping away from God, the psalmist enters God's presence and finds a new perspective, allowing him to stride forwards.

Join us on this journey to discover and know God who, as the psalmist says, is the 'strength of my heart and my portion for ever' (Psa. 73:26).

Every Day *with Jesus*

NOV/DEC 2016

A New Perspective

'But as for me, it is good to be near God. I have made the sovereign LORD my refuge' Psalm 73:28

Be revived and refreshed by God's Word   CWR

Also available as eBook/ eSubscription

OBTAIN YOUR COPY FROM
CWR, a Christian bookshop or National Distributor.
If you would like to take out a subscription, see the order form at the back of these notes.

Steadfastness

FOR READING & MEDITATION - LUKE 8:4-15

'But the seed on good soil stands for those ... who hear the word,
retain it, and by persevering produce a crop.' (v15)

Our text for today in *The Message* paraphrase reads, 'But the seed in the good earth–these are the good-hearts who seize the Word and hold on no matter what, sticking with it until there's a harvest.' Notice the words 'sticking with it until there's a harvest'; they teach us that only the faithful are finally fruitful.

The minister of a large church, when asked what was the outstanding need of his congregation, replied, 'Faithfulness.' He went on to say, 'Fifty per cent of my church members are hangers-on who are getting a free ride and contributing nothing from purse or person. Twenty-five per cent promise to do something and then, after a few stabs at it, drop out. They lack fidelity. The life of this church is carried on by the remaining twenty-five per cent.' Another great preacher said: 'If we could get people who put their hand to the plough to decide that they will never draw back no matter what the wind or weather, what a powerful Church we would have.' Powerful indeed. It's so sad that because we do not persevere the Church is not what it could be.

How many of us, I wonder, are guilty of failing or reneging on promises and only half fulfilling tasks? It cannot be an issue of the Holy Spirit, for He dwells in us to provide the strength and energy to see things through – if we let Him. Success in this is achieved by surrendering to the Spirit who is already resident in us. As someone once put it, 'The Christian life is not my responsibility, but my response to His ability.' I tell you, never is the work of the Holy Spirit demonstrated more wonderfully than when it is seen in the lives of those who are faithful.

FURTHER STUDY

1 Sam. 15:1-26;
1 Pet. 5:10

1. What did Saul half fulfil and what was the result?

2. What will God's grace achieve?

Father, I recognise yet again that the fruit of the Spirit can develop in me only to the extent that I am surrendered. Help me go more deeply into You, this day and every day. In Jesus' name I pray. Amen.

FOR READING & MEDITATION – MATTHEW 11:20-30

'Take my yoke upon you and learn from me, for I am gentle and humble in heart' (v29)

We come now to the eighth fruit of the Spirit – gentleness or meekness. The original Greek word *prautes* is translated in various ways in different translations of the New Testament. One version uses the word 'tolerance', another 'forbearance' and another 'adaptability'. This Greek word has no exact equivalent in English, and, after examining the words used in the different translations, my personal opinion is that the Good News Bible gets closest to the true meaning when it uses the word 'humility'.

The words 'humble' and 'gentle' are found together a number of times in the New Testament, as, for example, in our text for today: 'I am gentle and humble in heart.' (Other examples include Ephesians 4:2 and Colossians 3:12.) The mature Christian in whom the Spirit dwells is a person who is gentle and humble. It has been said that apart from love, nothing is more characteristic of a Christian, and nothing more caricatured and misunderstood than humility. Generally, the world has not had much time for gentleness or humility. 'Throughout the ages', says one writer, 'it is a virtue that has not been greatly praised – except by a few.'

To understand the true strength humility calls for it is helpful to look at how *The Message* paraphrase describes gentleness: 'not needing to force our way in life'. A lady once came up to me at the end of a Bible study I had just given on humility and said, 'I do love to hear a preacher expound the subject of humility. You see, it is one of my greatest qualities, and I want to know as much as I can about it.' I felt that sadly, by highlighting her humility, she was showing that this quality was probably lacking in her life.

FURTHER STUDY

Matt. 18:1-5;
Mark 9:35-37;
Eph. 4:1-2

1. How is greatness shown in the kingdom?

2. How do we live a life worthy of our calling in Jesus?

Lord Jesus Christ, my Saviour and my Redeemer, I long so much to be like You – gentle and humble. And as I seek to walk the path of humility, help me not to lose my way. In Your dear name I ask it. Amen.

FOR READING & MEDITATION - PHILIPPIANS 2:1-11
'Your attitude should be the same as that of Christ Jesus' (v5)

Yesterday we said that the strength of humility has not been truly recognised – except by a few – in any age. Ancient writers regarded the quality of humility as a 'servile, grovelling spirit'. People today seem to view it in the same way and confuse it with the obsequious spirit of Uriah Heep, the character in Charles Dickens' novel, *David Copperfield*, remembered for the words, 'I am so very 'umble, Master Copperfield.' Indeed William Ewart Gladstone, one of Britain's past prime ministers, once said, 'Humility as a sovereign grace is the creation of Christianity.'

FURTHER STUDY

Mark 10:35-45;
1 Tim. 1:12-17;
1 Cor. 15:9

1. What is Jesus' example?

2. How did Paul regard himself?

Though we have chosen 'humility' as the best word to define the eighth fruit of the Spirit, we must be careful not to miss the thought that is contained in some of the other words used by translators, such as gentleness, meekness, forbearance, adaptability and tolerance. Together they create a picture of this fruit of the Spirit as a gentleness that does not need to force its way in life but has a joyous desire to serve.

Humility is not only misunderstood by the world; it is, I believe, misunderstood by the Christian Church. Some confuse it, for example, with self-belittlement. They think that by denigrating themselves or putting themselves down they are acting in humility. But by deliberately setting out to make themselves small they are in reality trying to make themselves big. Self-effacement is their way of gaining face. They take the lowest place simply in order to be invited to go up higher. They express derogatory opinions of themselves in the hope that they will be contradicted. This is not real humility; this is feigned humility, which is an unworthy substitute.

Father, clarify my understanding so that I can discern between true humility and feigned humility. Help me to have a mind that is open to Your mind so that I comprehend all things clearly. In Jesus' name. Amen.

FOR READING & MEDITATION - JOHN 13:1-15

'Jesus knew that the Father had put all things under his power ...
he poured water ... and began to wash his disciples' feet' (vv3,5)

This passage of Scripture has long been one of my favourite sections of the New Testament. Listen to some verses from it in the New King James Version translation: 'Jesus, knowing that the Father had given all things into His hands, and that He had come from God and was going to God, rose from supper and laid aside His garments, took a towel ... poured water into a basin and began to wash the disciples' feet' (vv3–5). It was the consciousness of His standing in the Father that enabled His humility. The small dare not be humble.

Let me explain what I mean by 'standing'. Jesus' standing was rooted in God. Being in God made Him great – and humble. Great because humble – humble because great. A Hindu remarked to a missionary, 'I used to believe in idols but now I don't believe in them at all. I am coming round to the belief that I myself am a god.' He gave up his idols and made one of himself! When we lose sight of God we lose sight of humility. It is as simple as that: no true vision of God – no true vision of humility.

As we said yesterday, humility is not a cringing, servile attitude, although sadly many Christians seem to view it in this way. Phillips Brooks, a nineteenth-century American preacher, once said, 'The true way to be humble is not to stoop until you are smaller than yourself, but to stand at your real height against some higher nature that will show you what the real smallness of your greatness is. Stand at your highest, and then look at Christ, then go away and forever be humble.' The truly humble are conscious of His greatness before they are conscious of their own humility.

FURTHER STUDY

Num. 12:1-11;
Exod. 18:13-16

1. Contrast Miriam and Aaron's attitudes with that of Moses.

2. How could Moses be humble yet lead and judge a nation?

Lord God, in my effort to understand humility please help me always to remember that it springs from a consciousness of greatness. And may my sense of greatness be rooted in You. In Jesus' name. Amen.

'A sane view of oneself'

FOR READING & MEDITATION - ROMANS 12:1-8

'Do not think of yourself more highly than you ought,
but rather think of yourself with sober judgment' (v3)

We continue attempting to clear up some of the misunderstandings that surround the word 'humility'. Humility has often been confused with that debilitating state that has been described as an 'inferiority complex'. But however much humility and an inferiority complex may resemble each other – and we have to admit that there are similarities – humility is significantly different. Humility is neither the result of childhood deprivations nor is it a mental health issue. And it is not derived from an unhelpful comparison with other people. Humility is seeing ourselves from God's point of view and having a right opinion of ourselves.

FURTHER STUDY

1 Sam. 17:26-36;
1 Chron.
29:10-16

1. How was David's view of himself different to others?

2. What did he acknowledge that revealed his true humility?

Paul urges us in the passage we have read today not to think of ourselves more highly than we ought, 'but to think soberly, as God has dealt to each one a measure of faith' (v3, NKJV). This verse is sometimes interpreted as meaning that we should cultivate a low opinion of ourselves, but look again at what the apostle is saying: 'Do not think of yourself more highly than you ought, but rather think of yourself with sober judgment.' We should not think of ourselves more highly than we ought, but, by the same token, we should not think of ourselves more lowly than we ought. We need a sane and balanced estimate of ourselves – one that is neither too high nor too low.

Humility is rooted in a correct view of God, but it is also fixed in a correct view of ourselves. These two facts need to be emphasised in today's Church for I am convinced that a large percentage of Christians have neither a correct view of God nor a correct view of themselves.

My Father and my God, I pray once again that You will give me a clear insight into this issue. Help me have a true understanding of You for then I shall have a true understanding of myself. In Jesus' name. Amen.

Humility - a teachable spirit

MON
24 OCT

FOR READING & MEDITATION - JAMES 1:17-27

'humbly accept the word planted in you, which can save you.' (v21)

Some Christians confuse humility with lack of ambition but here, too, they are mistaken. Christians in whom the harvest of the Spirit is being reaped may or may not lack worldly ambition, but in the spiritual area of life they are exceedingly ambitious. And why? Because their hearts are not set on human status symbols such as titles, honours, awards, distinctions or money but on God Himself. If these things are bestowed upon them then they regard them as a trust; they are not, however, the things they covet. For them, life reaches its fulfilment not in things of the earth but in God.

Having spent our time so far focusing on what humility is not let us now focus more directly on what it is. 'Humility', said William Barclay, 'is a gentle, gracious and submissive spirit.' He went on to suggest that in order to understand humility properly we need to look at five significant passages of Scripture. When we have looked at all five, we shall then have a composite picture of this beautiful virtue which the Holy Spirit seeks to bring to fruition in our lives.

The first is from today's passage: James 1:21, which *The Message* puts beautifully: 'In simple humility, let our gardener, God, landscape you with the Word, making a salvation-garden of your life.' Humility is a teachable spirit – an attitude that recognises our own limitations and accepts the fact that without God's help we cannot understand the depths of truth. Every Christian who has a good understanding of Scripture will, to some degree, be humble, for those who approach the Bible with a proud and know-all attitude will find it firmly shut and it will not reveal anything to them.

FURTHER STUDY

2 Kings 22:11-20; Dan. 5:18-30

1. How did King Josiah humble himself?

2. Contrast Belshazzar's response to that of Josiah.

Heavenly Father, give me a teachable spirit - especially in relation to Scripture. Help me to lay aside my own ideas when I come to Your Word so that I might be able to absorb Your ideas. In Jesus' name I ask it. Amen.

How to deal with opposition

FOR READING & MEDITATION - MICAH 6:1-8

'And what does the LORD require of you? To act justly and to love mercy and to walk humbly with your God.' (v8)

Another passage to look at if we are to understand the full meaning of humility is Galatians 6:1: 'if someone is caught in a sin, you who are spiritual should restore him gently.' Paul's advice is that if someone has committed a particular sin they should be approached in a spirit of humility. Restoration can be offered in a way that discourages or in a way that sets a person on his or her feet with the determination to do better. Humility is the spirit that makes restoration an incentive and not a reason to be disheartened, a means to hope and not a cause of despair.

FURTHER STUDY

1 Thess. 2:7-12;
2 Tim. 2:24-26;
Titus 3:1-2

1. How did Paul relate to others?

2. What were his instructions to believers?

The third scripture William Barclay suggested is 2 Timothy 2:25: 'Those who oppose him he must gently instruct.' Paul is saying here that when we encounter those who disagree with us, and whom we think to be mistaken, we must not attempt to 'hammer' them into changing their minds but treat them with the utmost gentleness and respect. Suppose we go into a room on a bitterly cold day and find the windows are frozen on the inside. We can either try to rub away the ice on the inside of the window panes, or we can light a fire in the grate or turn on the central heating and allow the window to clear itself. Heat does quickly what rubbing may take a long time to do. When dealing with those whom you believe to be in error or mistaken, always remember that gentle humility will accomplish what no amount of battering could ever do.

There is a story about the sun and the wind competing to get a coat off a man's back. The wind did its best but the man held his coat more tightly around him. Then the sun came out and it was not long before the man took off his coat.

Father God, I sense that the ways You teach me through Your Word are also written in me. I am at my best only as I follow You. Help me, dear Lord, always to follow You in the path of humility. Amen.

FOR READING & MEDITATION - PROVERBS 18:1-13

'Before his downfall a man's heart is proud, but humility comes before honour.' (v12)

The fourth scripture we look at to discover more about what humility is is 1 Peter 3:15, which reads, 'Always be prepared to give an answer to everyone who asks you … But do this with gentleness and respect.' Real Christian witness always has a gracious humility and gentleness about it, which is far more effective than the aggressive approach of those who attempt to force people to accept the gospel message.

The final text we look at is James 3:13: 'Who is wise and understanding among you? Let him show it by his good life, by deeds done in the humility that comes from wisdom.' The real highlight of a life that is pleasing to God is a humble and quiet spirit. Those who think they are not gifted by temperament to relate to people with gentleness and humility need not despair. The Spirit who dwells in you will, if you allow Him, transform your temperament so that it becomes increasingly Christlike. Paul's spiritual progress may be measured by the fact that in 1 Corinthians 15:9 he says, 'I am the least of the apostles.' Writing later to the Ephesians, he says, 'I am less than the least', not now of the apostles but 'of all God's people' (Eph. 3:8). Still later, when writing to Timothy, he says that 'Christ Jesus came into the world to save sinners – of whom I am the worst' (1 Tim. 1:15). Oh, the wonder of humility. God declared through Isaiah, 'I dwell … with him who has a contrite and humble spirit' (Isa. 57:15, NKJV).

James said, 'God opposes the proud' (James 4:6). Do you realise what that means? God repels the approaches of the proud. As Psalm 138:6 tells us, the proud He knows only from afar; it is to the humble that He gives grace.

FURTHER STUDY

James 3:13-18; 1 Pet. 5:1-7

1. What is the relationship between deeds, humility and wisdom?

2. Who receive God's grace and favour?

Lord Jesus, I can have too much of many things but I cannot have too much of You. I cannot be too much like You or have too much of Your Spirit. Please fill me to overflowing so that I become more and more like You. Amen.

Christ-empowered living

FOR READING & MEDITATION - PROVERBS 16:20-33

'Better a patient man than a warrior, a man who controls his temper than one who takes a city.' (v32)

Now we come to the last of the nine qualities of the fruit of the Spirit – self-control. Underlying the word is the idea of self-restraint, a fine mastery of one's personality, a controlled and disciplined nature. When the Holy Spirit is at work in our lives He not only gives us the power to do what we should but also the power not to do what is wrong.

It is noteworthy that Paul puts self-control last. Most systems of thought, both ancient and modern, would put it first. Consider the various philosophies that have fascinated people over past centuries and what do you find? They have all sought to produce a happy and contented person through self-control. Some have advocated thought-control, some breath-control, others will-control. The Christian way is different – it produces joyful and contented people, not primarily by thought-control or even will-control, but by Christ-empowered living.

Christians are people who are self-controlled, 'able to marshal and direct our energies wisely' (*The Message*), not by self-effort alone but through the gracious work of the Holy Spirit who lives within us. We do not gain the things of the Spirit through self-control; we gain self-control through the presence of the Spirit in our lives. You see, if we begin with self-control then we are the centre – we are controlling ourselves. But if we begin, as Paul did, with the first fruit of the Spirit – love – then the spring of action is outgoing and we are released from self-preoccupation. When we begin with love, we end with self-control, as the Holy Spirit cultivates the fruits in our hearts. But it is not a nervous, anxious self-control; it is a control that is natural and unstrained.

FURTHER STUDY

2 Sam. 11:1-17, 26-27

1. Contrast Uriah's self-control with David's lack of it.

2. What was the Lord's view of David's actions?

Gracious Father, help me grasp the thought that self-control is the result when Jesus is in control. When You are in control You empower me for life. It is indeed beautiful. Thank You, dear Father. Amen.

Choose your cause

FOR READING & MEDITATION – MATTHEW 6:24-34
'But seek first his kingdom and his righteousness, and all these things will be given to you as well.' (v33)

Some people attempt to live the Christian life through self-control rather than through love, and quickly discover that it does not work. I myself tried to be a Christian this way. There was a time in my teens when I was greatly attracted to Christianity, but was unwilling to make the full surrender that it so clearly advocates. Every day I would start out with the intention that I would do everything in my power to keep myself from sin – and every night I fell into bed feeling a failure. How could a diseased will heal a diseased soul? Then I surrendered my life to Jesus and something wonderful happened – His love flowed into my heart, and as I began to love Him all lesser loves dropped away.

A university professor, writing on the subject of loyalty, said an interesting thing: 'There is only one way to be an ethical individual and that is to choose your cause and then to serve it. This central loyalty to a cause puts other loyalties in their place as subordinate. Then life as a whole is co-ordinated because all lesser loyalties are subordinated.'

Translate his thinking into New Testament language and you find an interesting similarity. The 'cause' we choose is Jesus and His kingdom, and when we seek them first, all other things, including self-control, are added to us. This does not mean that once we become Christians we automatically become people with complete control of the things that go on within us. We have, of course, that potential, but in practice it becomes a reality only as we root and ground ourselves in Jesus. Submitting to Him allows the Spirit's fruit, including self-control, to develop and grow. What a way to live!

FURTHER STUDY

Neh. 6:1-4;
1 Pet. 1:13-16

1. How did Nehemiah's cause save him from harm?

2. What do we set our hopes upon?

Lord God, I am so thankful that when I threw my will on Your side, You threw Your will on my side. I am controlled because I am under control. Amen.

Danger areas of life

FOR READING & MEDITATION - PROVERBS 15:1-14

'The tongue that brings healing is a tree of life, but a deceitful
tongue crushes the spirit.' (v4)

What are some of the areas of life in which we need to
have self-control? Areas where we need to direct our
energies wisely? Let me highlight what I consider to be the
three most important. The first is the area of sex. Within
the boundaries of God's design, sex is wonderfully creative
and satisfying, but when sex is unrestrained and without
boundaries it becomes chaotic, often resulting in difficult
and complicated consequences.

Within the marriage relationship, which is where God
designed sex to be, there is need for self-control too. If one's
partner becomes the means of self-gratification
instead of a person to be loved and respected then
disrespect sets in. You cannot use another without
abusing yourself. Your attitudes towards another
become your attitudes towards yourself. If you use
another for sexual purposes then sex uses you. Sex
is a dedication or it is a desecration, and when it is
a desecration it becomes degradation.

**FURTHER
STUDY**

1 Cor. 6:12-20;
James 3:1-12

1. How can we
honour God?

2. How does
James say we
keep our bodies
in check?

Another area of life in which we need the self-
control that the Spirit provides is the tongue.
James points out that the tongue is an important
indicator of how well we control ourselves (see
James 3:2–12). It has been said that there are three stages in
verbal communication: impulse, consideration and speech.
Many omit the second and jump from impulse to speech.
The person who has self-control pauses between impulse
and speech and gives time for consideration. The Holy Spirit
– if we let Him – comes to our aid to help us be sure that
what we say is what we ought to say and not something
we blurt out without thought. This is true of everyone –
extroverts included!

**God, help me to be a disciplined person in thought, word and deed.
And help me to know when to hold my tongue and when to speak.
In Jesus' name. Amen.**

FOR READING & MEDITATION - 1 CORINTHIANS 9:19-27

'I beat my body and make it my slave so that after I have preached
to others, I myself will not be disqualified for the prize.' (v27)

A third area of life in which we need self-control is that
which has to do with our own bodies. The body, by its
very nature, is comfort-loving, but too much comfort is
debilitating and we need to cultivate a healthy lifestyle. The
mother of John Wesley is reported to have said, 'Whatever
increases the strength and authority of your body over your
mind, however innocent it may be in itself – that thing is
sin to you.' David Hill, a Christian writer, puts it this way:
'There is before each one of us an altar of sacrifice, unseen
but real and present; and on this altar we are called to offer
ourselves. There is some crucifixion of the flesh,
some physical self-sacrifice, the abandonment of
some bodily indulgence which the spirit of man
knows that he is called to make.'

**FURTHER
STUDY**

Rom. 13:11-14;
Col. 3:1-14

What are some of the things our bodies clamour
for? One is food, and generally speaking, those
of us who live in the West eat far more than is
good for us. Another thing the body clamours for
is sleep. People differ in the amount of sleep that
they need, and too much sleep can be as unhelpful
as too little.

1. What desires
do we need
to control?

2. Where do we
set our minds
and hearts?

How delighted we are with the luxuries of life.
It has been said that the luxuries of one generation become
the bare necessities of the next. We should be cautious not to
go too far down this road and regard the body as an enemy
that has to be continually afflicted, but, if we are thoroughly
honest, most of us will admit that self-control is a fruit we
most definitely need. Self-control helps the Christian to offer
to God a responsive personality that is not cloyed by comfort
or impassive from indulgence but sensitive to guidance and
ready to live according to His perfect will.

**Lord Jesus Christ, once again I ask that You dwell deep within
me by Your Spirit and help me to be free from the strong desires
that would cancel out my effectiveness. This I ask in and through
Your peerless and precious name. Amen.**

A portrait of a saint

FOR READING & MEDITATION - GALATIANS 5:13-26

'Since we live by the Spirit, let us keep in step with the Spirit.' (v25)

The Christian in whom the fruit of the Spirit is matured gives the best portrayal of saintliness it is possible to find. How would we go about painting a portrait of a saint? Some sections of the Church say that a saint must have several qualifications – faith, hope, love, wisdom, a sense of justice, fortitude, self-restraint – and all of them in large measure. Others take from Scripture the catalogue of the virtues produced by the Holy Spirit. They see, therefore, in Paul's list an inspired catalogue of the qualities that characterise a saint.

FURTHER STUDY

Gal. 5:22-23;
2 Pet. 1:3-11

1. How can we participate in the divine nature?

2. Memorise, and continue to meditate on, Gal. 5:22-23.

How, then, does God go about painting a portrait of a saint? His canvas is the heart of one who is redeemed. The colours He puts on His palette are love, joy, peace, patience, kindness, goodness, faithfulness, humility and self-control. The absence of any one of these virtues would be serious, for every one is needed if the portrait is to be a masterpiece. And these colours are not pastel shades – each one is deep and rich and vibrant. The model He uses is the peerless example of His own dear Son, in whom every quality is seen to perfection and wonderfully balanced by every other.

Even now, as you read these lines, His brush is at work, gently and lovingly caressing into your nature all the lineaments of Jesus' character. All He asks is that you hold still – that you stop trying and start trusting. Do this and, in the truest sense of the word, you will become a saint. Have you been repeating Galatians 5:22–23 and meditating on it daily over the past weeks as I suggested? Good. Now continue to meditate on these verses regularly. It could revolutionise your Christian life. Try it and see.

My Father and my God, help me hold still as You go about the task of using my life to create the portrait of a saint. Let every brush stroke reflect the beauty and loveliness of Your eternal Son. In Jesus' name. Amen.

ORDER FORM

4 EASY WAYS TO ORDER:

1. Phone in your credit card order: **01252 784700** (Mon-Fri, 9.30am - 5pm)

2. Visit our online store at **www.cwr.org.uk/store**

3. Send this form together with your payment to:
   CWR, Waverley Abbey House, Waverley Lane, Farnham, Surrey GU9 8EP

4. Visit your local Christian bookshop

or a list of our National Distributors, who supply countries outside the UK, visit www.cwr.org.uk/distributors

YOUR DETAILS (REQUIRED FOR ORDERS AND DONATIONS)

Full Name: CWR ID No. (if known):

Home Address:

                                           Postcode:

Telephone No. (for queries):   Email:

PUBLICATIONS

TITLE	QTY	PRICE	TOTAL
		Total publications	

All CWR adult Bible-reading notes are also available in eBook and email subscription format.
Visit www.cwr.org.uk for further information.

UK p&p: up to £24.99 = **£2.99**; £25.00 and over = **FREE**	
Elsewhere p&p: up to £10 = **£4.95**; £10.01 - £50 = **£6.95**; £50.01 - £99.99 = **£10**; £100 and over = **£30**	
Please allow 14 days for delivery Total publications and p&p **A**	

SUBSCRIPTIONS* (NON DIRECT DEBIT)

	QTY	PRICE (INCLUDING P&P)			TOTAL
		UK	Europe	Elsewhere	
Every Day with Jesus (1yr, 6 issues)		£15.95	£19.95	Please contact nearest National Distributor or CWR direct	
Large Print Every Day with Jesus (1yr, 6 issues)		£15.95	£19.95		
Inspiring Women Every Day (1yr, 6 issues)		£15.95	£19.95		
Life Every Day (Jeff Lucas) (1yr, 6 issues)		£15.95	£19.95		
Mettle: 14-18s (1yr, 3 issues)		£14.50	£16.60		
YP's: 11-15s (1yr, 6 issues)		£15.95	£19.95		
Topz: 7-11s (1yr, 6 issues)		£15.95	£19.95		
Cover to Cover Every Day		Email subscription only, visit online store.			
Total Subscriptions (Subscription prices already include postage and packing) **B**					

ase circle which bimonthly issue you would like your subscription to commence from:
n/Feb Mar/Apr May/Jun Jul/Aug Sep/Oct Nov/Dec

Only use this section for subscriptions paid for by credit/debit card or
cheque. For Direct Debit subscriptions see overleaf.

CONTINUED OVERLEAF >>

PAYMENT DETAILS

☐ I enclose a cheque/PO made payable to CWR for the amount of: £ _____

☐ Please charge my credit/debit card.

Cardholder's Name (in BLOCK CAPITALS) _____

Card No. ☐☐☐☐ ☐☐☐☐ ☐☐☐☐ ☐☐☐☐

Expires End ☐☐☐

Security Code ☐☐☐

GIFT TO CWR ☐ Please send me an acknowledgement of my gift **C** ☐

GIFT AID (YOUR HOME ADDRESS REQUIRED, SEE OVERLEAF)

giftaid it

I am a UK taxpayer and want CWR to reclaim the tax on all my donations for the four years prior to this year **and on** all donations I make from the date of this Gift Aid declaration until further notice.*

Taxpayer's Full Name (in BLOCK CAPITALS) _____

Signature _____ **Date** _____

*I am a UK taxpayer and understand that if I pay less Income Tax and/or Capital Gains Tax than the amount of Gift Aid claimed on all my donations in that tax year it is my responsibility to pay any difference.

GRAND TOTAL (Total of A, B, & C) ☐

SUBSCRIPTIONS BY DIRECT DEBIT (UK BANK ACCOUNT HOLDERS ONLY)

Subscriptions cost £15.95 (except *Mettle*: £14.50) for one year for delivery within the UK. Please tick relevant boxes and fill in the form

☐ *Every Day with Jesus* (1yr, 6 issues)
☐ Large Print *Every Day with Jesus* (1yr, 6 issues)
☐ *Inspiring Women Every Day* (1yr, 6 issues)
☐ *Life Every Day* (Jeff Lucas) (1yr, 6 issues)

☐ *Mettle*: 14-18s (1yr, 3 issues)
☐ *YP's*: 11-15s (1yr, 6 issues)
☐ *Topz*: 7-11s (1yr, 6 issues)

Issue to commence f
☐ Jan/Feb ☐ Jul/Aug
☐ Mar/Apr ☐ Sep/Oct
☐ May/Jun ☐ Nov/Dec

CWR

Instruction to your Bank or
Building Society to pay by Direct Debit

DIRECT Debit

Please fill in the form and send to: CWR, Waverley Abbey House,
Waverley Lane, Farnham, Surrey GU9 8EP

Name and full postal address of your Bank or Building Society

To: The Manager _____ Bank/Building Society

Address _____

_____

_____

Postcode _____

Name(s) of Account Holder(s)

_____

Branch Sort Code

☐☐ ☐☐ ☐☐

Bank/Building Society Account Number

☐☐☐☐☐☐☐☐

Originator's Identification Number

4	2	0	4	8	7

Reference

☐☐☐☐☐☐☐☐☐☐☐

Instruction to your Bank or Building Society

Please pay CWR Direct Debits from the account detailed in this Instruction subject to the safeguards assured by the Direct Debit Guarantee.
I understand that this Instruction may remain with CWR and, if so, details passed electronically to my Bank/Building Society.

Signature(s)

_____

_____

Date _____

Banks and Building Societies may not accept Direct Debit Instructions for some types of account